Rolling Pennies in the Dark

Rolling Pennies in the Dark

A Memoir with a Message

DOUGLAS MACKINNON

HOWARD BOOKS
A DIVISION OF SIMON & SCHUSTER, INC.

NEW YORK NASHVILLE LONDON TORONTO SYDNEY NEW DELHI

Howard Books
A Division of Simon & Schuster, Inc.
1230 Avenue of the Americas
New York, NY 10020

First Howard Books trade paperback edition November 2012

HOWARD and colophon are trademarks of Simon & Schuster, Inc.

For information about special discounts for bulk purchases, please contact
Simon & Schuster Special Sales at 1-866-506-1949 or business@simonandschuster.com.

The Simon & Schuster Speakers Bureau can bring authors to your live event.
For more information or to book an event, contact the Simon & Schuster Speakers
Bureau at 1-866-248-3049 or visit our website at www.simonspeakers.com.

Designed by Akasha Archer

Manufactured in the United States of America

10 9 8 7 6 5 4 3 2 1

The Library of Congress has cataloged the hardcover edition as follows:

MacKinnon, Douglas.
    Rolling pennies in the dark : a memoir with a message / by Douglas MacKinnon.
        p. cm.
    1. MacKinnon, Douglas   2. Authors, American—20th century—
Biography.   3. Journalists—United States—Biography.   4. United States—Officials
and employees—Biography.   I. Title.
    PS3563.A31764Z46 2012
    813'.54—dc23   2011041284
    [B]

ISBN 978-1-4516-0788-8
ISBN 978-1-4516-0789-5 (pbk)
ISBN 978-1-4516-0790-1 (ebook)

For my mom and dad
I do still love you and I do miss you.
Hopefully, we will get your long-awaited love and hugs in Heaven.

CONTENTS

PART TWO: A Message

PART ONE

A Memoir

1

A Stabbing Precedes the Gunfire

It really *does* hurt to get stabbed.

I had just landed a punch to the side of a rival's head. As he yelped in pain and fell out of the way, I felt a hand grab me by the right shoulder and spin me completely around. A millisecond after completing the turn, I saw a knife blade arching up toward my midsection. I instinctively turned sideways to shield my stomach and chest. While successfully protecting those vital areas, I was not able to avoid the force of the blade.

The tip of the switchblade, which entered the minuscule muscle of my skinny thirteen-year-old bicep, immediately struck calcium. A white haze of pain filled my eyes, as my lungs sucked in enough oxygen to let out an earsplitting scream.

The *reason* I got stabbed in the first place was that some of my friends and I were involved in an old-fashioned *West Side Story*–type gang fight. Back in the day, in my never-dull corner of the Dorchester section of Boston, it was not about what neighborhood you were from but which street you lived on. Some friends and I met up with some territorial individuals from a rival street, and before anyone knew what was happening, it was on.

Since this was circa 1969, and we weren't yet smart enough to call ourselves a "crew" and carry "nines" or "Mac-10s," this instant and fierce disagreement was waged with pipes, boards, fists, and the occasional knife. Unfortunately for me, I didn't get hit with a board, pipe, or fist.

I got stabbed. I was the victim of a very violent crime at a very early age. But when I thought about that episode a few months later, I knew that between myself and the older kid who stabbed me—he was sixteen and already a career criminal—I was, by far, the more fortunate. I say that for three reasons.

First, simply and most important, I was able to spin my stomach and chest away from the blade and take the strike in the arm. This particular rival was not trying to frighten me or wound me. He meant to kill me.

Second, about one second after I was stabbed, one of my buddies caved in this guy's chest with a five-pound cobblestone rock. The collision between rock and human body was not pleasant. While I never got all the details, I think the contact was enough to break a bone or two and send him to Boston City Hospital. A facility that—at least at that time—made medieval practitioners of the dark arts look advanced by comparison. Having been to that alleged center of healing a few times already in my young life, I knew better than to go back—even if blood was pouring out of a large hole in my tiny arm.

Ignorance is sometimes a wonderful thing. Having never been stabbed before, I did not know enough to assign the knife wound the importance it deserved. To me, it was no big deal. Like everything else in my life, I'd just fix it myself.

I just took my shirt off, wrapped it around the dripping hole in my arm, ran the few blocks back to our apartment, went into the bathroom, unwrapped the now blood-soaked shirt, and poured some of my father's rubbing alcohol directly into the cut.

Mistake.

My sister, who was sitting outside at the time, told me you could hear my scream several streets away. Fortunately, my parents, who were already in a vodka-induced coma in their bedroom, never heard a thing. After screaming from the shock of the alcohol and almost passing out on the bathroom floor from a pain that seemed much worse than the actual stabbing, I pinched the cut closed as tight as I could, put some folded toilet paper over it, and then used a couple of feet of white hockey tape to secure my battlefield bandage in place. While archaic, I still felt it was better than whatever treatment my attacker eventually received in that dungeon of a hospital.

The third reason I felt I was the luckier of the two of us was that not long after this guy was discharged from Boston City and recovered, I was told he was found shot in a local park.

His demise is what my friends and I fought off almost every single day as we trolled the streets and alleys, desperately trying to stay one step ahead of those determined to hurt us.

As I tried to recover from the physical and mental pain of my knife wound, the only things I had going for me at the time were a tremendous chip on my shoulder—which pertained to just about everyone—some inherited natural intelligence, and a PhD in street smarts. I had no intention of giving *anyone* the satisfaction of seeing me fail.

I was born in a hospital in Dorchester, Massachusetts. At the time, Dorchester was an ultratough, blue-collar section of Boston, filled with mostly wonderful, hardworking people; it's a place I will always be proud to call home.

Dorchester was never the problem. Poverty, homelessness, and hopelessness were the problems; and they were manufactured by two people—and two people only—our "parents," John MacKinnon and Marie Carmel MacKinnon. These two individuals were not only full-blown alcoholics, but complete hedonists who saw their three emaciated and damaged children as obstacles to be crushed on their egocentric path to self-destruction.

By the time I was seventeen, our family had moved a total of thirty-four times. For those of you who, like me, are not fond of math, that's an average of once every six months. *None* of the moves were voluntary—some, in fact, were quite disturbing and violent.

2

A Two-Year-Old's
Introduction to Poverty

M y first memory that something was not quite right was implanted in my mind when I was about two and a half years old.

We were living in a suburb on the South Shore of Boston, and the winter's first snow had arrived. Even at that age, I was fascinated by the weather; so as soon as I spied the very first snowflake, I was begging my brother to let me run outside so I could see, feel, and taste it.

I have few memories from that time of my parents. I mostly remember my brother, Jay, who was a little less than two years older than me. At around four years of age, he was the only "adult supervision" I had.

As we ventured out into the snow, we had nothing resembling proper winter clothing. No coats, no boots, no hats, no mittens.

For some semblance of warmth, Jay put an extra shirt on me. Beyond that, we put socks over our hands. Dirty, smelly socks at that. It was all we had.

My introduction to snow, poverty, and the cruelty of children all came within minutes of running onto the front lawn and laughing happily as I slid, slipped, and fell atop this wonderful, cold white blanket. As Jay and I threw snowballs, made snow angels, and tried to build our very first snowman, a couple of older kids—maybe five years old—came over to join us.

As they began to talk to us, they almost immediately focused on the dirty socks covering our hands. They started laughing and singing something like "smelly mittens, smelly mittens. You're wearing smelly mittens."

Jay was more mild-mannered than I was and just ignored them and kept on playing. I did not. I began trying to hit and push them, all the while crying because they were making fun of me.

When I eventually ran back into the house, I have no memory of my mom coming to comfort me or give me a hug. Rather, the only memory I have is of sitting down on the broken and tattered linoleum floor in our kitchen as I continued to cry silently to myself.

3

Me, Baby Jesus, and My First Crime

During my third year on the planet and as we bounced from decrepit place to decrepit place, my baby sister, Janice, was born. Because of our nomadic lifestyle and crippling poverty, my sister and brother were the only children I ever interacted with for any consistent period of time; consequently, they were the only "friends" I had. That was about to change.

I was in the first grade and on the late end of five years old. My parents had enrolled my brother and me in a parochial school in a suburb of Boston. The school was down the street from where we lived, and during my very first day there, I came upon a display of religious symbols and trinkets resting on a table outside the main office of the school. Symbols and trinkets, as it turned out, that were for sale.

As I walked past the table festooned with various Catholic and Christian objects, my eyes were instantly drawn to a tiny Nativity scene made out of plastic, which showcased Mary, Joseph, and the Baby Jesus. I was mesmerized, and for reasons I did not and do not understand, found tremendous comfort in its simple but beautiful—at least to me—presentation.

The colors of the tiny Nativity scene were vivid and warm. I especially remember the blue of Mary's shawl and the smiling face of Baby Jesus.

When I hurried off to my class and asked my homeroom nun if I could have it, she answered, "No." She then smiled down at me and announced that I "could buy it."

At five, I didn't understand what "buy it" meant. I guess after seeing the confused look on my face, the nun explained that I would have to go home and ask my parents for the money needed to purchase the beautiful little Nativity scene.

When I still looked back up at her with uncomprehending eyes, she said, "You give us four quarters, and we will give you the Nativity scene."

Oh. Four quarters. Why didn't she say so in the first place? I knew what quarters were. And better than that, I knew just where to find some.

Still excited after running all the way home, I went looking for my mom and dad and found them both snoring heavily in their bedroom. After several attempts to wake them, I gave up and decided the only way I was going to get that Nativity scene was to liberate the money.

Like most men of that era, when my dad did leave the house for "work," he always wore a suit. One day, while playing hide-and-seek with my brother and sister, I hid in my mom and dad's bedroom closet. As I did, I bumped into the suit coat my dad had worn that day, and I heard the distinct and always pleasant chime of coins clanging against each other. Upon inspection, I found that my dad had a large supply of quarters in the small change pocket within the larger side pocket of his suit.

Other than discovering them that day, I did nothing. I did not take even one. I knew what stealing was, and I knew it would be wrong to take the coins without asking.

Weeks later, I again took notice of the Baby Jesus at my school and sparked an instant bond with that tiny little replica. Not with the plastic face or the mold, but with the inherent goodness, purity, and spirituality of what that smiling tiny face represented. I felt a connection and more than that . . . inexplicably, I felt like I had found a friend.

While only five, I was still a deep little thinker. I looked at *everything* from every possible angle, mostly, I think, because life had already taught me to look for the traps or the danger in every situation, and it became a survival technique hardwired into my mind.

Because of that, I remember walking out of my mom and dad's room and sitting on the dirty mattress on the floor of our bedroom, pondering the situation. Why was I so intrigued by the Nativity scene? Why did I feel better, and even a bit safer, just looking at it? And then I thought . . . what if somebody else got it instead of me?

I needed to get to that Nativity scene and buy it before some other kid did. That meant only one thing: I had to go back to the closet in my mom and dad's room and take four quarters from my dad's suit pocket.

And that's exactly what I did. My clandestine operation was a success. The next day, the first thing I did—even before going to my homeroom—was to run to the table outside the main office to see if *my* little Nativity scene was still there. Joyfully, it was. I next stepped over to the nun manning the table and handed over my four quarters.

She took the money and wrapped my new treasure in white paper and placed it in a small paper bag. I had never been so happy. I clutched that bag to my chest for the rest of the day.

Ironically, my first real introduction to Baby Jesus coincided with my first crime. And if not a crime, then at least a sin of some sort—a sin I instantly hoped Baby Jesus would forgive.

As soon as school was over, I ran all the way home and went straight to our bare and depressing little bedroom so I could place—and hide—my little Nativity scene in the far corner of our bedroom closet.

Once it was situated there, I found an electric Christmas candle and placed it on the floor next to the Nativity scene. When I plugged in the candle and it actually worked, I could not have been more proud or happy as I watched the soft white light bathe Mary, Joseph, and now *my* little Baby Jesus in its warm glow. A warm glow, in a dark and filthy closet, that enveloped me and my new friend with at least a modicum of peace and serenity.

My tiny Baby Jesus was my new and *only* constant friend. A friend who was always there for me. Always listened. Who always smiled back up at me from the center of that warm glow of light anytime and every time I ran to him when I was hurt beyond words, when my world was once again turned upside down by the extreme poverty and dysfunction that was our family.

My little plastic Baby Jesus was the very first solid foundation for my two uncertain feet, which were anchored to spindly legs below my bony and malnourished body.

4

In Desperate Search of Gold
at the End of the Rainbow

At the "mature" age of six, I was fully aware that things were
not good between my mom and dad. They fought, they
yelled, they smashed vodka bottles against the wall and floor, and
they often did so in front of the three of us.

One day in particular, I remember my mom screaming about
our lack of money and then running into her room, where she
proceeded to cry loudly behind the now-slammed bedroom door.

My mom's dad—my grandfather George McNeil—happened
to be staying with us during one of his rare but always welcome
and wonderful visits.

He—along with my Baby Jesus—was one of my true sources
of comfort. Constant among the evictions, the pain, the never-
ending hunger, and the squalor were his smile and concern, and
most of all, his kindness and understanding of situations well beyond our years.

As my mom, his only child, screamed and carried on behind
her closed bedroom door, my grandfather gently herded the three
of us out into the backyard and out of earshot of this latest parental
train wreck.

A thunderstorm had just passed over the tree line of the woods behind our home, and there in the distant sky, a vivid rainbow appeared.

My grandfather wiped down the tattered lawn chairs in our backyard and had us sit. My baby sister, Janice, and I squeezed into one chair and Jay took the other.

Once we were seated, my grandfather pointed at the rainbow over the woods. "There is magic in that rainbow," he said with a wink and a spreading smile.

I looked at the rainbow from one end to the other to see if I could see what was so special about it.

"I don't see anything, Papa," I said in disappointment.

"That's because you can't see it from here."

"Why?" I asked while staring even harder at the rainbow.

My grandfather again pointed to the multicolored bridge in the sky. "Because it's at the very end of the rainbow. That's where they hide it."

"Who hides what?" Jay asked.

"The little people. The leprechauns. And what they hide at the end of the rainbow is a pot of gold coins. *Real* gold coins."

My six-year-old eyes instantly went as wide as one of those coins.

"Real gold?" I asked in wonder.

"Real gold," my grandfather answered as he laughed and tousled my hair.

Days after my mom had retreated to her bedroom to cry about our lack of money and my grandfather had sadly ended his visit, I walked out to our backyard and, sure enough, spotted another magnificent rainbow. Remembering my grandfather's story—and driven by empathy, imagination, and the realization that I could only count on myself—I decided the *one way* I could help my mom and our family was to find the end of that rainbow and dig up the pot of gold.

We lived in a sparsely populated area with the dense forest behind our home. To my six-year-old eyes, it seemed the end of that rainbow came down smack in the middle of those woods.

Without telling a soul, I took off at a sprint for the woods. My grandfather had told us that the leprechauns liked to tease the "big people" and would turn off the rainbow so its end and their treasure would not be discovered.

While running through the dense forest and thick underbrush, I tripped over a tree root and tumbled down a pretty steep ravine. When I stopped cartwheeling down the side of the hill, I realized that my face, arms, and hands were cut and bleeding, after going through some kind of sticker bush, and that my little body was bruised as well. Had my head hit one of the large rocks on the way down, the animals would have had their way with me long before my mom and dad knew I was missing.

After getting my bearings and slowly climbing back up the ravine and walking to a nearby clearing—where I thought the rainbow ended—I discovered that it was gone and that the leprechauns had, indeed, turned it off.

Crying now from both the cuts and bruises and from my disappointment at not finding a way to ease my mom's pain, I headed home. Of course, when I got there, my fear was realized. No one other than my brother and sister knew or cared that I had been gone.

Upon seeing me, eight-year-old Jay took me by the hand and led me into the kitchen, where he did the best he could with napkins and water from the faucet to clean my cuts and wash my dirt-, blood-, and tear-streaked face.

5

Crashing a School Bus for My Sister

Soon after my tumble down the ravine and while I was still in the first grade, we were evicted and had to move yet again. This time to an even more remote and rural setting of New England, into a home straight out of an underfunded Halloween movie.

It was especially scary living there because not another house or human could be seen from our house and because—since we had no electricity—the blackness of the nights were only dented by the candles we were given by our parents as our sole source of light . . . and heat.

Soon after we had moved there, my brother, sister, and I were playing hide-and-seek in the total darkness of the upstairs level after waiting the required amount of time for our parents to pass out from drinking their funny-smelling "water."

Except . . . when we snuck out into the hallway, it was not in total darkness. Far from it. From the partially opened door that led to our parents' bedroom, we saw a bright yellow flickering light dancing about the room.

When my brother and I tiptoed down the hallway and poked our heads into their bedroom, we noticed that they were, in fact, passed out in their bed. Nothing unusual about that.

What did grab our attention, however, was that one of them

had knocked a lit candle onto the bed, and one corner of the sheet and mattress was now on fire.

As Jay ran to try to wake them from their deep sleep, I ran down to the bathroom in the middle of the hallway and filled my sister's red plastic beach bucket with water.

When I got back to the bedroom, Jay had managed to drag our still passed-out mom out of the bed and onto the floor. As he continued to pull her across the bare wooden floor, I hurried over to the growing flames and threw the bucket of water at them.

While all of this was going on, our father did not even stir, as he blissfully snored away.

Once we were sure the fire would not restart, we left them where they were: my mom sprawled out on the floor next to the bed and my dad in the middle of the bed with his head no more than three feet from the scorched and blackened corner of the mattress.

As I looked at them, anger grew within me. While our parents were in the same house with us physically, at three, six, and eight years old, we were about as alone as three children could be.

Worse, actually. If we had really been all alone, we would have been much safer, with less risk of the three of us burning the house down with us in it.

Part of being alone meant that my brother and I had to get ourselves up and ready for school. Part of getting ready was scrounging to find something to eat for breakfast. Our first priority was to at least make sure our little sister had some food.

Unfortunately, our cupboards were almost always bare except for the multitude of cockroaches that scattered every time we opened the doors—in the foolish hope that *this* time, maybe we would find food.

More often than not, breakfast for the three of us consisted of a few saltine crackers and some brownish tap water that had a strong metal aftertaste and particles that stuck to our tongues. It was that or the always-popular nothing.

At eight and six, Jay and I had already morphed into surrogate protectors of our baby sister, with me taking the more active role. Janice and I had been soul mates since the day she could first talk. As such, I felt and knew it was my obligation to keep her from as much harm as possible. With that belief ingrained into my little mind, I especially hated the thought of her being all alone with our parents when Jay and I were at school. As the candle incident proved, she could be—and was—in grave danger.

Who would look after her? Who would keep her company? Who would protect her? Once Jay and I left for school, the answer was *no one*.

When we left, our three-year-old sister was truly on her own with no parental or adult supervision. On top of that, she was in a large, dark, creepy, and decaying house with no electricity and no phone.

My brother and I were the first ones to be picked up on the bus route, so we had to be at the bus stop at seven-thirty. We walked down a long dirt road that led to a small paved road; oftentimes, my three-year-old sister would walk with us to the bus stop and then when we pulled away, she would walk back by herself to that isolated and unlit house.

Depending on the day, our parents either didn't care that she was walking back alone down a quarter-mile stretch of dirt road, or were passed out from a heavy night of drinking and had not a clue. Either way, it was madness.

For Jay and me, it was just life as we knew it. Better that she was with us for a little longer before she had to go back to the house to be alone with our parents.

In anticipation of the bus arriving on this small paved road in the middle of nowhere, we would have Janice wait on the other side near the dirt road while Jay and I stood across the street, about ten or fifteen feet away and next to the tree where the bus would stop. That way, we could still talk to her, but she would not have to cross the street after we left.

After Jay and I boarded the yellow school bus, we would both turn from inside the bus and wave good-bye to our baby sister. As the bus started to pull away on this particular morning, I noticed that Janice was crying and had not turned to head home.

I was sitting in the first green bench seat behind the driver, with Jay across the aisle from me in his seat. At this point, it was just me, Jay, and the bus driver.

I turned from looking at Janice to tap the bus driver on his back and ask him to please stop the bus.

In a very unfriendly way, he said "No," and kept driving the bus down the small paved road toward his next pickup.

I turned around to look back at my sister and then pointed her out to Jay. He looked at Janice and then at me and basically shrugged his shoulders as if to say, "I know, but what can we do now?"

I turned back in my seat and tapped the bus driver a bit harder on the back and asked him to stop the bus. I wanted and needed to get off that bus to find out what was wrong with my sister.

This time, the bus driver yelled at me as he raised his right arm off the wheel in a somewhat threatening motion.

As I was only six, I employed the next best way I knew to get the attention of an adult. I started crying loudly while begging to be let off the bus.

That tactic did not work, either. In fact, it only made him angrier, and he screamed at me, "Shut up!"

I turned back to look for my sister and saw her still standing there but quickly receding into the distance.

Desperation took over, and I went for what I felt was my final option.

As an undersized, underfed, skinny six-year-old, I climbed up on top of the seat behind the driver and jumped from it to the top of his head and his very large shoulders.

Once there, I wrapped one arm around his throat and the other around his eyes and then held on for dear life. I have a distinct memory of Jay trying frantically to pull me off the driver as the bus started to weave back and forth across the road.

I did get my way . . . but only after the bus drove into a ditch by the side of the road and came to an abrupt halt.

The bus driver screamed wildly at me and kicked both me and Jay off his bus, telling us we "could never come back on." I couldn't care less.

As soon as I was off, I was running back up the road to find my sister and find out what was wrong.

When I reached her, I gave her a hug, and when she finally stopped crying, she said she was scared.

"Mommy and Daddy don't come out. I want to go with you."

I tried to explain as best I could that she could not come with us yet because she wasn't old enough for school. I was terrified for her safety but didn't want to scare her even more.

I told her that for now, after Jay and I left for school, she was to go back to our room and stay there. I told her to play and talk with her dolls and that they would be her friends until we got home from school. I both ordered and begged her never to come out of that room unless she heard Mommy's and Daddy's voices, and they were actually walking around.

Even at my young age, no one had to tell me we had an abnormal, miserable existence and that my little sister was paying the highest price of all.

6

A Grandmother's Love
and a Peek at Normalcy

My first real memory of my grandparents' loving home was of us arriving on their front porch in the dead of the night. We had just been thrown out of our home, and Nana and Papa MacKinnon's smiling faces greeted us as they quickly ushered us in from the cold.

Once inside, my grandmother gently guided the three of us upstairs and toward the bathtub at the far end of the hallway.

As my grandmother ran the bath for our baby sister, I heard the booming voice of my six-foot-three, 250-pound grandfather echoing up from the living room. He was yelling at my mom and dad, with most of the angry words directed at my dad . . . his oldest child.

As the lecture continued downstairs, my grandmother plopped our sister into the warm, clean water of the tub and soon had Jay and I repeating the exercise.

I don't know if I smiled up at my grandmother or not, but my first reaction was pure joy as Jay and I sank into the warm water. Since our family almost always existed without either electricity or heating oil, or both, we almost never had hot or even warm water.

Worse, it always seemed that in whatever horrible place we were living for the moment, the water that did come out of the faucet was not only very cold, but also very dirty.

Nana handed me a little yellow rubber duck to play with, and I don't think I had ever felt so safe or so happy.

Once out of the tub and dried with big, fluffy towels, we quickly got our next special surprise. Our grandmother handed us brand-new underwear and brand-new pajamas to put on. Jay and I broke out in grins as we got dressed and while our Nana dressed Janice. In our young lives, we had never had a pair of new pajamas before. Never. We had always gone to sleep on our dirty mattress on the floor either in our soiled underwear or in the clothes we had on that day, which were always dirty.

I still remember the three of us touching each other's pajamas as we continued to smile in delighted shock at the new material, the cleanness of it, and its new-clothes smell. Nana then trooped the three of us down to her kitchen, which always gave out the most mouthwatering aromas, and she sat us at the table and fed us.

As we devoured whatever she put in front of us, I caught her giving Papa some kind of look as she shook her head and began to cry.

Once we were finished with our food, Nana redirected us back upstairs to the bathroom, where new toothbrushes and toothpaste awaited us. This was also a relatively new experience for us, as most nights we put ourselves to bed and usually never brushed our teeth, either because we did not know better or because we had no toothbrushes. Now, under the loving gaze of our grandmother, we proudly brushed our neglected teeth as best we could.

The next and last surprise of the night may have been the best. We were going to sleep in real beds with real pillows. More than that, they were real beds with clean sheets, clean pillowcases, and clean blankets.

At least for one night, the three of us would not have to share a dirty mattress on the floor. At least for one night, we would not go to sleep hungry. At least for one night, we were clean and had on clean underwear and pajamas.

At least for one night, all of our dreams came true.

Over the course of these early years, we showed up on our grandparents' front porch a number of times, at all hours of the day and night.

On one of those nights, we were hand-delivered to our grandparents' home by our uncle Peter—my dad's youngest brother—who had literally rescued the three of us from the backseat of a frozen car covered in snow, just as we were checking out from hypothermia.

As my uncle Peter relates the story, my parents had driven themselves and us back to Dorchester and my grandparents' house, because it was again the middle of winter and we had been without heat, electricity, and food for days in our suburban home. At the time this happened, I was about four, Jay about six, and our baby sister, Janice, a little less than one.

When my parents got all of us to my grandparents' home, my dad told his tale of woe. At the strong prodding from my grandmother, my grandfather very reluctantly gave him the money needed to buy heating oil and food for all of us. With cash now firmly in hand, my mom and dad packed us all back into the car for our drive back to suburban Boston.

Unfortunately, along the way, my alcoholic parents spotted a bar that was still open during the snowstorm. They immediately pulled in front, shut off the car, and with the blizzard raging, told us they would be right out.

Several hours later, at closing time, they phoned my grandparents again to shamelessly confess that they had spent all the cash *just* given to them on booze for themselves in the bar.

Now outraged, my grandparents decided the only thing to do was to send their youngest child, Peter, back out in the storm to collect the three of us and bring us back to the warmth, safety, and sanity of their home.

When Uncle Peter finally made it through the deepening snow in the dark of the night, he quickly found my parents drunk at a table in the back of the bar. When he didn't see my brother, sister, or me at the table, Peter started shaking my father as he screamed, "Where are the kids? Where are *your* children?"

Peter says that at this point, some of the very tough locals still left in the bar looked over at my parents in growing anger at where this was leading.

After a few more shakes, my father slurred out, *"I think . . . maybe still in the car."*

In shock, Uncle Peter and a couple of the locals ran outside and finally located our now totally buried car. After some frantic digging, they got our listless forms out of the backseat and rushed us into the warmth of the bar. My less-than-one-year-old sister was in her bassinet and in the worst shape.

As my uncle and the manager of the bar were desperately trying to figure out if we were going to survive the experience, some of the other men in the bar tried to attack my father for this criminal neglect, which almost resulted in the loss of our lives.

7

Sunday Dinners and My Escape
from the Kids' Table

When we were lucky enough to spend a weekend at my grandparents', the absolute highlight for me—aside from the new and clean everything—was Sunday dinner.

Sunday dinner at my grandmother's meant that whichever of her children and their spouses were in town would be at the dinner. As my grandparents' adult children were intelligent and interested in politics and world events, these dinners were always lively affairs.

In fact, to my awakening intellect, their interest in politics and the world around them seemed to be driven by my grandfather Michael MacKinnon. For as long as I could remember, there were always political signs in my grandparents' front yard supporting some local Democrat. While far from liberal, my grandfather was a proud, hardworking John F. Kennedy Democrat.

So, no sooner did the adults start to butter their rolls than the discussion would turn to politics. And when that happened, I would start to come out of my shell and experience traces of happiness.

I was *clean,* I had on *brand-new* clothes, and I was in a room where every single person—with the exception of my parents—

loved me unconditionally. I could be myself—a child who could never stop asking "why" or trying to figure out every mystery before me.

It was during those times that the proverbial wallflower bloomed. Even when I was six or seven, I wanted to sit at the table with the adults. I *never* wanted to sit at the card table with the other kids. The card table was for babies, and I was there to talk politics, science, spaceflight, and whatever else was going on in the world. And so, by hook, by crook, or more likely by constantly whining, I usually ended up at the magical adult table, where the world was talked about in detail.

After my grandparents, the next two people who had the most positive impact on my life and who sat at that table were two of my uncles: my already mentioned uncle Peter MacKinnon and my uncle Tom MacKinnon. Peter was the baby of the family and Tom was the second youngest.

Because Peter was just thirteen years older than my brother, Jay, we considered him more of an older brother than an uncle. He and his older brother, Tom, meant the world to my sister, my brother, and me.

As much as outsiders *could* know—which meant seeing only the tip of the dysfunctional iceberg that was our home life—Peter and Tom knew the horror we lived through as kids and did as much as they could to help us escape . . . at least for a few hours at a time.

My uncle Tom was a wonderful man and, anytime we lived in or visited Dorchester, always managed to take me, Jay, and Janice out to a movie. One Halloween, he even took us late-night trick-or-treating when he found out our parents had not taken us out and had not bought us costumes.

My uncle Tom was a very special person and a bit of a lost soul in his family. As a young boy, he had a condition that caused most of his hair to fall out. Children, being children, made fun of him constantly and caused him to withdraw.

For whatever reason, when he was with the three of us, he could relax and just be himself—an exceptionally good human being who only wanted to help others.

In us, he found three tiny misfits who, like him, did not conform to the rules of society. Because of that, he found as much pleasure taking care of us as we did in his enormous kindness.

8

My Little Project and the Effects
of Too Much Alcohol

Uncle Peter was an outdoorsman, and two of his "things" were shooting and fishing. As a small boy, I loved the shooting part, but just hated the fishing. I didn't want to hurt the fish. I didn't want to hurt *any* animals. Ever. The same couldn't necessarily be said about human beings, however . . . at least bad ones.

Peter had taught my brother and me to shoot at a very young age. When I was eight, I had regularly fired a .22 rifle as well as a few shotguns.

Speaking of those shotguns, Jay got acquainted with Peter's double-barrel twelve-gauge shotgun in a memorable, shocking, and quite funny way. In a field somewhere in Rhode Island, our twenty-three-year-old uncle was teaching us firearm safety and how to fire his shotguns. After his instructions, Jay, who was ten and abnormally thin from constant malnutrition, got down on one knee and decided to pull *both* triggers of the powerful shotgun at the same time. Why, I have no idea.

Since he weighed about as much as a wet cat, Newton's Third Law instantly took over, and Jay cartwheeled backward about six times from the force of the blast. There was a lesson learned.

• • •

Later that same day, I got my own lesson: alcohol abuse and senti-mentality don't mix. Not at all.

At the age of eight, I was building and tearing apart anything and everything. One of the things I built at the time was a little wooden stand for my mom to put her flowers on. It stood about a foot or so high and, through my eight-year-old eyes, looked pretty professional. I had sawn the pieces, sanded them down, nailed them together, and then varnished the whole thing.

I had shown my creation to Uncle Peter upon his arrival, and several hours and a few cans of beer later, he asked me to go get it. I was so proud. One of my favorite uncles wanted to see my little project again.

I ran as fast as I could into our temporary home and brought it back to him, breathless from running and with excitement that an adult member of my extended family was truly impressed with my work.

Uncle Peter took the stand from my hands, patted me on the head, and then walked my creation about fifty yards into the field in front of our home. Once he picked out a spot, he put my hand-built stand on the ground, finished his beer, and then put the empty beer can on top of my stand. Why would he do that? I wondered.

He then walked back to where my father—his oldest brother—was sitting in his own sea of empty beer cans. He and my dad picked up their rifles and, over the course of the next few minutes, turned my beloved handmade stand into a pile of splinters.

As they laughed at their marksmanship and the result, I cursed the effects alcohol had on my beloved little project.

But in the end, it was okay. A splintered little stand was a small price to pay for the massive amount of love and support given to us by our uncle Peter.

9

JFK's Assassination and an Eviction

This particular school day seemed not much different than any other. I had left for school from a home with no electricity or phone, and very hungry as usual.

The only thing different about that morning was that my mom seemed more disoriented and nervous than normal, since my dad had pulled one of his disappearing acts and had not been seen or heard from in days.

Later that day, I was in my third-grade homeroom class daydreaming and staring out the window at the clouds when suddenly there was an announcement over the loudspeaker saying that President John F. Kennedy had been shot in Dallas, Texas. *What?*

For some reason, the kid sitting at the desk to my right started to laugh. As soon as he did, I hauled off and punched him in the arm as hard as I could. This got me immediately carted off to the principal's office to be disciplined.

As to why I would hit my fellow classmate . . . well, it made perfect sense to me. It was actually more of an involuntary reaction produced by years of benevolent brainwashing than anything malicious on my part.

Everybody in my family had a love of politics and seemed to be a Democrat—even my parents when they were sober. And more than that, they were *Boston* Democrats, which meant that without reservation, they worshiped the ground that John F. Kennedy trod.

As an eight-year-old, I had been told over and over that my ancestors had come from Scotland, to Nova Scotia, then down to Boston, and that my grandfather Michael MacKinnon—who moved from Nova Scotia to Boston at a very young age—had always considered himself as much Canadian as American. So much so that he became president of the Canadian American League, and one of his first duties and orders had been to organize strongly for John F. Kennedy.

Proud evidence of that relationship could be seen in a black-and-white picture of my grandfather and then senator John F. Kennedy on display in my grandparents' living room. Senator Kennedy was wearing a simple but elegant tuxedo, and looked like a man of confidence who had the ability to lead.

My grandfather was wearing a well-tailored gray suit that covered his huge frame. Senator Kennedy and my grandfather were shaking hands on a stage in Dorchester in 1957, and John F. Kennedy's hand was basically swallowed up by my grandfather's huge but gentle paw.

As such, politics was the topic of discussion at almost every dinner at my grandparents' home, with President Kennedy named the best politician ever. By this time in my life, I thought President John F. Kennedy was Santa Claus, the Easter Bunny, and the Tooth Fairy all rolled into one.

So when the kid next to me laughed, I swung as hard as I could.

After getting lectured by the principal—who didn't really have his heart in the lecture and, I think, was secretly happy that I hit the offender—I left school and started my half-mile solitary walk back home.

As I started to get closer to our house, I was confronted with a very strange and scary sight. Everything we owned—which was never very much—was strewn across the sidewalk in front of the house. Everything. When I got closer still, I found my mother sitting in a chair amid all the chaos, sobbing uncontrollably.

Knowing something was beyond wrong, my eyes filled with tears, and by the time I reached my mom to hug her, I was sobbing as well.

Through her tears and with vodka-scented breath, my mother explained that because my father had gone missing and had failed to pay the landlord his money for "a very long time," the police and some movers had come to "drag" her out of our home and dump all of our meager possessions on the sidewalk.

So, the night of the day John F. Kennedy was assassinated, I was living in a car with my mother, sister, and brother, terrified by an eviction process, which was about to become the norm for a number of years.

Soon after that particular and memorable eviction—and several others that quickly followed—I started to fantasize about living in a very sad place. A storage shed. An *actual* storage shed where people with their very own homes and their very own manicured lawns would keep their very own lawn mowers, tools, trash cans, and other items.

Janice and I decided that we would most especially love to live in one of those storage sheds that was built to look like a miniature barn. We thought that would be wonderful.

At ages eight and five, we talked all the time about how we would decorate the interior of the eight-by-ten-foot shed. We planned the color we would paint the outside and what color the trim would be. We imagined that it would be filled with food, clothes, lights, and our own TV. After we had it all constructed and stocked in our damaged minds, we would discuss which of our imaginary friends would be invited over.

But mostly, we dreamed of just having this small shed to call home. To have an actual permanent home from which no one could evict us. Where no one would hurt us anymore. A home we would live in so we wouldn't be forced to sleep in a car or a cheap, filthy, cockroach-infested, and dangerous motel for the uncounted time.

I picked out and dreamed of this storage shed because I thought it would be something my brother, sister, and I could buy with paper-route, shoe-shine, and bottle-deposit return money, or even build on our own after running away from home.

While my dream of living in a storage shed never became a physical reality, it was real in my mind, and I hid out in it often.

10

A Book Provides Escape
While Planting a Seed

My introduction to novels and the written word came when we were riding somewhere in my dad's big, old, white Cadillac convertible with red leather seats. My dad believed in only driving used, huge, heavy Cadillacs or Lincolns. That's all he ever owned. That's all he ever drove. Dangerous weapons indeed when he passed out at the wheel and veered across the double-yellow going about eighty miles an hour.

On this particular ride in "Vodka One," my dad was driving as usual, my mom was sitting next to him, and my brother, sister, and I were sitting in the back on the huge red leather bench seat.

I usually sat behind my dad, Janice sat in the middle, and Jay, behind my mom. No particular reason for the seating order, except for my sister being in the middle. She was the youngest, so she got the "hump." Something all cars had back then.

As we were driving, I noticed a hardcover copy of *The Wizard of Oz* lying on the floor at my feet. Having nothing better to do than watch my dad's head slip closer and closer to the steering wheel on the way to a drunken mini-coma, I picked up the book and started reading the first page. By the end of the night, I had finished the entire book.

For me, it was magic. By reading *The Wizard of Oz* by L. Frank Baum, I was able to magically and instantly transport myself far away from the hunger, dirt, and uncertainty that were my life. Because of the talent and gift of an author, I was able to immerse myself in written words that possessed a very real and tangible healing power. To me, it was nothing short of a minor miracle.

As long as there were words on a page, I had the opportunity to travel back in time, across vast oceans, to mythical lands, or into outer space. I had the chance to escape and give my battered mind a much-needed reprieve.

Even at eight, I was fully aware that, even though my parents were irresponsible, irrational, inebriated, and a rapidly growing threat to us as well as themselves, they were two very intelligent people. I had often been told by my grandparents and uncles that by every standard of the time, my dad had the IQ of a genius, with my mom holding her own in the brains department. Fortunately for me, to complement that severely wasted intelligence, they both had a real love of books.

When sober, my dad was an insatiable reader. He could and often did read five books a week. My mom was less of an avid reader; she averaged one book about every week or two.

To my eternal gratitude, this love of the written word was passed down to me through osmosis. Reading kept me sane during the years of pain. Words and books helped me to cope. I have zero doubt about that. So, after zipping through *The Wizard of Oz,* I snuck off with any novel I could find in the house that I thought might interest me.

About the same time that I figured out that books and the written word could lighten the load of my troubled mind, I learned how to employ another critical survival technique.

I mastered the skill of killing my happiness. I had experienced so much pain and constant disappointment that I decided the only way to survive was to basically *murder* the hope of happiness for myself.

I remember staying up late one night watching someone on our small black-and-white TV who was reading children's letters to Santa Claus. Some were funny. At the end, the host of the show said he was now going to read letters from some very, very poor children.

Each letter from a poor child like me was the exact same. These very poor kids *only* asked Santa for presents for their mom, dad, brothers, and sisters. *Never* for themselves. Ever. They begged Santa to bring something, *anything,* to those they loved. These poor children even said that as long as their family members got something, they would be happy with nothing.

The man on TV—who was crying after he read the last letter—said these selfless children were the *real* little angels on Earth.

I did not know or understand much about angels, but I knew that the protection and happiness of my sister and brother gave me a purpose and set me on a path I was anxious to navigate.

While I had killed the hope of happiness for myself, I desperately wanted to provide at least a sliver of it to my sister and brother.

11

Poor Public Schools for Me . . . Please

I became quite angry at my parents for enrolling me in "good schools." Granted, these Catholic schools were clearly superior academically to the poor public schools in the area, but many of the kids who attended them picked on me every single day.

All of the kids who were mean to me always wore new clothes, always had their hair cut, were always clean, and always had money for lunch. Every day, in the cruelest of ways, some of my classmates informed me how dirty I was, how bad I smelled, and that I didn't belong in *their* school. How right they were.

While many of the kids at these "good" schools made my life as miserable as possible, a few of the nuns actually took great pity on my brother, sister, and me. They did so by simply feeding us. We had no idea how bad we looked or what horrible condition we were in. We thought it was normal to go days without food and then live off the potato chips and packs of Kool-Aid our parents would throw on the kitchen counter before going to their room to pass out.

Many times after school, a couple of the nuns would take us into the rectory and give us hot soup and sandwiches. We would gobble them up in seconds and be given more by the nuns, who shared very knowing and sad looks.

We were getting used to those looks from adults.

• • •

I also found out that not only did God make imperfect people, but that He made imperfect nuns, too. Some, like the nuns who fed us, were wonderful; others were not.

One, in particular, I nicknamed "Sister Mary-Crazy." She was teaching English one day, trying to demonstrate how to indent a paragraph. For whatever reason, no matter how many different ways she explained it, I had no idea what she was talking about.

On many of my school days—maybe because of the lack of food, my advanced malnutrition, and the insanity at home—I was very tired and could not focus. I was even weak in the knees at times.

No matter the reason, on this day I just could not figure out what she meant by my "indenting a paragraph."

A few days before this exercise, Sister Mary-Crazy stood me in front of the whole class so she could point out how dirty I was, how "bad my body odor was," and that no one should ever come to school looking or smelling like me.

As soon as I returned to my seat, the other kids in class were laughing at me and pointing. The second the class was over, I ran down the hallway as fast as I could, burst out the front doors of the school, and escaped deep into the nearby woods, where I sat atop a fallen tree and screamed and cried until there was no more water or salt in my system.

Now, a few days after that ugly episode, Sister Mary-Crazy was at it again. This bear of a nun, who looked more like a man to me, was standing over my desk, looking down at me as she slapped a ruler with metronomic regularity into the palm of her left hand. As she did, I got so nervous that instead of "indenting" the para-graph, as I was now being *screamed* at to do, I was putting giant spaces between each word *in* the paragraph.

For some reason, my nervousness and lack of understand-ing seemed to infuriate Sister Mary-Crazy. As she leaned down to watch me put giant spaces between each word of the paragraph, she suddenly and violently grabbed me by the back of my neck, pulled me out of my chair, dragged me to the front of the class, and then slammed my forehead and face against the slate blackboard.

This "Woman of God"—as my grandmother always called them—hit my forehead against the blackboard with such force that a bump grew instantly on my head, and I collapsed to the floor as I saw stars and everything went fuzzy.

When I finally stumbled home, my parents were nowhere to be found. My head continued to pound, and the bump continued to grow until it split my skin. I had no idea what to do to help myself. I was scared.

I wanted to call my Nana, but like almost always, our phone was not working. My thinking was fuzzy, and I couldn't walk straight.

Finally, I wet a paper towel and got my little Nativity scene. I placed the Nativity scene next to the mattress on the floor, then I fell onto the mattress and put the wet paper towel on my bump and the cut in the center of it, and fell into a sleep.

A few weeks later, while at that same school, they were actually about to do something that made me quite happy. They were planning to show a Disney movie in the auditorium. Because I rarely got to go to a movie and because we almost never had a working television at home, I really looked forward to these films.

The school had already shown *Pollyanna* and *Johnny Tremain*. On this particular day, they were going to show a movie called *The Prince and the Pauper*. It sounded like it would be fun. It was not.

As I had absolutely no friends in the school, I took my usual seat by myself in the last row of the auditorium. I always felt better if my classmates could not see—or smell—me. If they could not see or smell me, they could not pick on me.

A few minutes into the movie, some of the meaner kids figured out what a pauper was. They instantly started looking around for me. When they spotted me in the back, they yelled, "Hey, MacKinnon. I didn't know you were in this movie. Except the beggar kid is better dressed than you, and we can't smell him on the screen."

Those comments and that treatment went on for weeks after they showed the movie. How much better off I would have been in a poor public school.

At the age of eight years, I realized that I was truly on my own.

12

A Nine-Year-Old Fires a Weapon in Self-Defense

Reconciled with the frightening reality that I really was on my own and that solutions and survival were all up to me, it was eviction time again.

We were uprooted from the latest depressing area and found ourselves deposited in an even more depressing area somewhere in New Hampshire. Our near-shack had four small rooms, and the walls were literally made out of some kind of thick cardboard. It was the most dreadful and remote place we had ever lived.

Our cardboard shack was miles from any other home and on the edge of a dirt road that led to a lake, which was a favorite drinking and making-out spot for the local white trash teenagers. These criminals-in-training would usually stop their cars in front of our house on the way back from a night of drinking and mating and throw beer cans and beer bottles at our front door and windows and absolutely petrify my mother and little sister in the process.

My mother, and not my dad, because when we lived in this desolate and dismal place, he was almost never around. It was just my mom, me, Jay, and Janice. Nothing really new there.

Little did these trespassing and terrorizing thugs know that, while we may have been in the middle of nowhere, we were *armed*. Even my mom.

My brother and I each had a .22, single bolt-action rifle, and my mom had a .45 automatic pistol. Very scary . . . for a lot of reasons.

After yet another terrifying night of beer bottles smashing against our house and through our front windows, the state police showed up, and with a wink and a nod basically said, "If these juvenile delinquents officially step on your property, you have the right to defend yourselves by any means necessary."

Good enough for me. I was now nine years old and took complete control of the situation. I had a defined mission in my ongoing quest to look out for and protect those I most loved.

After the state policeman left, I had my mom back our white Cadillac convertible up to our front stairs so the headlights would be facing the dirt road. Next, I pushed down the button on the floor of the car that turned on the high beams. I then tied a string around the pullout light switch and trailed the string into our living room. Now, with one pull of the string, I could bathe any car full of threatening creeps in a cascade of ultrabright light.

Sure enough, around ten o'clock that night, these vermin showed up and once again started throwing bottles at our home. My mom had given Jay and me orders to "only fire your guns *over* their heads if they start trouble and only if one of them steps on our property."

That order was not good enough for me. Not by a long shot. We had been running scared our entire lives, and it made me sad and enraged beyond reason to have these lowlifes terrorizing my mom and baby sister.

As soon as they started screaming and swearing in front of our home, and with the empty beer bottles now smashing against our steps and *through* our front windows, I pulled the string on the car light switch, and it looked like they were sitting in daylight. If that shocked them, what happened next made them poop their pants.

One of the car creatures did, indeed, run onto our front lawn, and once he did, through our now open and broken living room windows, my mom, Jay, and I started slinging lead. It was like they happened upon "Ma Barker and her boys." Bam! Bam! Bam! Bam! Bam! The gunfire was *really* loud. My mom could fire continuously while Jay and I had to shoot, pull back the bolt action, insert a new round, and then fire again.

There had been at least two of the inbreds standing in our front yard throwing bottles at our home, but by the third shot, all you could see were their legs diving back into their car.

At that point, Jay noticed something very bad . . . at least in his mind. He saw that my rifle was not aimed *over* their heads as instructed, but instead, aimed more or less at the middle of the car. Just as I was squeezing off my shot, Jay shoved the rifle barrel up, and I missed my target.

"What are you doing?!" he screamed. "Mom said to shoot over their heads!"

Instead of answering, I ran out the front door and down to the now-empty dirt road. As their taillights were disappearing in the distance, I got off two more shots before my brother tackled me.

Since the police didn't show up the next day, I'm guessing I missed. But it wasn't for lack of trying. My fragile young mind was clearly teetering on the edge of a very bad place.

13

Ducking Bullets Fired by Our Mom

A few weeks after target practice with the creeps, Jay, six-year-old Janice, and I took our nightly place on our thin and worn mattress, which lay on the floor of our decrepit bedroom. My sister shivered beneath our old and stained blue blanket and urgently poked me on the shoulder, pleading with me to "tell a Devil-Dog and his band of Cutthroats story."

The very fact that my baby sister was begging me to tell her a story meant that she was in a bad place mentally. Very bad. I understood why. We never *ever* got a break. Every day was bad and the next one was often worse. We were never allowed to catch our breath.

But there was a reason my sister was even more depressed than normal. Earlier that evening, as she had done in the past, our intoxicated mother had marched the three of us out into what passed for a living room in the cardboard and tar-paper shack we were existing in on the edge of Nowhere, New Hampshire. She assembled us like an audience on the broken yellow sofa and said, "I'm going to kill myself now, and it's all your father's fault."

After the dramatic announcement, and once sure we were all looking at the tragedy playing out before us, she took a bottle of sleeping pills out of her purse and swallowed the entire contents, using vodka as the lubricant.

The first time she pulled this cruel and mind-altering stunt, the three of us burst into tears and ran desperately to her. We held her tight and begged and screamed at the top of our lungs, "Please stop, Mommy. Please stop. Don't go to Heaven."

After her dramatic "act," the three of us ran back to our bedroom to formulate a plan. My brother and I argued over which one of us could walk or run the fastest down the two-or-three-mile road to tell a neighbor that our mom had just killed herself. As we were talking, I finally got the courage to peek around the door and look at my mother on the sofa. *Gee,* I thought. *She doesn't look sick.*

As I kept watching, I saw her pick up her purse, put something in it, take a sip of the vodka that she always drank from a coffee mug, and then stagger toward the bathroom. The second the bathroom door closed, I tiptoed on my dirt-encrusted, ripped socks toward her abandoned purse. I opened it and found a full bottle of sleeping pills. I wasn't too young to know what this meant.

Fire drill over. Lesson learned. As an actress, my mother had a bright future. As a mother, she was a monster.

Every child needs the love and protection of a parent. I had always been proud of the fact that my mom and I shared a birthday—until I was about six, when it became sadly obvious that I was a birthday "present" she wished had never been born.

It wasn't until later that I discovered the real tragedy. You see, my mother, like my father, was incredibly smart—which sometimes led to devious behavior on a number of levels. She only put on her suicide show when she knew our phone had been turned off for nonpayment, so that my brother and I couldn't dial the operator and call for help. This made it all the harder, because each time she put on this macabre little show, we literally had no one to turn to. With my father on the road and a phone that could only be used as a paperweight, we were limited to audience members only. How could my mother subject her children to such a sick, twisted, and emotionally crippling ritual?

On this particular night, when she once again paraded us out of our room to perch on the dirty yellow sofa, we knew what to expect. However, knowing that Mom was crazy and most likely faking did not make it any easier. Especially for my sister, who could not completely comprehend the difference between real and pretend. Hence, her fragile mind directing me to tell her and my brother a "Devil-Dog" story.

"Devil-Dog and his band of Cutthroats" were characters I had created a year earlier when I was eight. I had gotten the name from a popular Hostess treat.

Because of the abject poverty forced upon us by our parents, we didn't have the entertainment outlets most kids had. So, to help keep us sane and somewhat distracted, I invented Devil-Dog. At least once or twice a week, while lying on the mattress on our floor, I would tell a Devil-Dog story, until one or both of my siblings fell asleep.

Hearing the tremble in my sister's voice, I was determined—as her older brother turned young head of the family—to tell the best Devil-Dog story of all time. My sister slept on the left side of the mattress, with me in the middle and my brother on the right. I turned toward her and began:

"On a very stormy night on the high seas, Devil-Dog and his band of Cutthroats have all they can handle just to keep their ship from breaking apart in the crashing waves. All of a sudden, from his perch on the bridge of *The Rusty Bucket,* Devil-Dog spots what seems like another ship off on the horizon. This ship . . ."

Just as a smile was beginning to creep over my troubled sister's face and her eyes were starting to close, a frightening and *loud* BOOM came from the direction of the living room. Then another and another and another.

With each BOOM, a hole was blown through the cardboard wall of our bedroom about three feet above our heads. And with each BOOM, my baby sister screamed in terror as she pulled the tattered blanket higher and higher up over her head.

Because Jay and I had .22 rifles and had been around guns a fair amount of time, we instantly knew what was going on. Our mother was on the other side of that thin cardboard wall emptying her .45 pistol into our bedroom. "She's trying to kill us!" I screamed above the pounding and echoing gunshots.

Still lying sideways, I grabbed my sister and pulled her into my chest as I held her down on the mattress. As I did, I yelled at Jay, "Stay down until she stops!"

The terror did not stop until she ran out of bullets. But a few seconds after our mother stopped shooting, my sister strangely returned to "normal." No more tears, no more screaming, no more shock.

Looking back, her behavior was symptomatic of the serious mental issues that haunted our young, developing minds. But, at six, nine, and eleven, we didn't have a clue. We just instinctively knew that we had to get ourselves back to "normal" as quickly as possible so we'd be ready for the next assault on our senses.

As a tormented nine-year-old whose mother had just fired a clip of .45 bullets that traveled through our bedroom wall, passed just above our heads, and then exited our bedroom through the far wall and into the woods behind our house, I immediately felt a number of things. But the most potent feeling was resignation.

All three of us felt the same thing. At our tender ages, we had experienced more pain than most adults endure in a lifetime and had become numb to the horrors that kept assaulting us. We were resigned to our fate.

To this day, I have no idea what my mom had in mind with her display of Annie Oakley–like marksmanship. In her deranged and drunken state, was she screaming out for attention? Was she really trying to shoot us? Was she trying to shoot herself and just kept missing? What?

Maybe the indignity of where she was living forced her to snap. The once white but now dirt-colored one-level shack we occupied had a tiny kitchen (with appliances that didn't work), a small living room, two small bedrooms, and holes in all the floors that gave us a view of the bare ground beneath and allowed vermin inside. Our "home" was situated near the end of a two-mile dirt road with absolutely no sign of civilization. While the three of us kids had no friends, we at least had each other. In my mom's damaged and vodka-altered mind, she was as alone as she'd ever been.

After being evicted from what was nothing more than a tenement in Manchester, New Hampshire, my father had conned somebody into letting us stay in this depressing dump in the middle of nowhere. He then deposited the four of us there and disappeared for days or weeks at a time. While he was gone, my mom would tell us that he was off "stealing money from hardworking people or out with one of his many girlfriends."

Uncounted insecurities and demons swirled inside my mom's mind, with most emanating from the fact that she had married a criminal, womanizing alley cat of a husband. And in her deranged state, she believed she was powerless to do anything about it because of her "incurable" love for her adored John. What she could not or would not take out on her awful, cheating husband, she took out on her innocent children. With a vengeance.

To be brutally poor is tough enough. To be brutally poor while those who brought you into the world do everything within their power to willfully and permanently cripple your psyche is a circle of Hell known to but an unfortunate few. My parents had domain over that circle, and we were their captive audience . . . for the moment. Never a day went by that I didn't tell my little sister of my next plan—no matter how far-fetched—to free her from our unrelenting horror and place her and us in a "normal" home.

As the three of us huddled under the blanket and held on for dear life, I could only surmise that with her fake pill-popping freak show exposed, my mom felt she had to max out the dial on the craziness meter to make her next statement. What better way than to shoot a bunch of bullets in the direction of your offspring.

By sheer coincidence, my father ran into the house as my mom dropped the now-empty .45 onto the bare wooden floor. While we were happy that he had staggered in to stop the madness, how much better if he had shown up *before* the first bullet split the air at over two thousand feet per second, as it turned our cardboard bedroom wall into Swiss cheese.

The three of us were still lying on our mattress when we heard our dad tackle our mom and felt the shack tremble as their combined body weight crashed to the floor of the living room.

It quickly dawned on me that the reason our bodies were not full of bullet holes was that we were on that mattress on the floor. As the majority of the bullets entered our room at "normal" bed height, had we been in a real bed and not on the floor, then "Ouch." The Lord does, indeed, work in mysterious ways.

Because the incomprehensible had become part of our everyday childhood, we learned at a very young age to lock the insanity into a tight little compartment in the back of our minds. Intuitively, we knew that if we did not perfect this art of the tortured, there was a very good chance we would not survive to reach adulthood. Or if we did, we'd wish we hadn't.

When the men in the white coats showed up to haul my mom away to an insane asylum, Janice and I went to that "special" place of invented normalcy. As they were fighting to squeeze her in a straitjacket, we were not upset, we were not crying, we were not concerned. Not one bit. Instead, when the strangers entered our cardboard home to take our mom away—for what we knew might be the rest of our lives—we instantly started to play a game. This particular game was to guess what the strangers looked like based only on the sounds of their voices.

"Are the men here to take Mommy away?" my baby sister asked.

"Yes," I answered, as I tried to listen to what was going on outside.

"How many of them are there?"

"Sounds like two," I said, as I turned my face toward the wall.

"Are they big men?"

"I think so. I think in their line of work, they have to be big in case the people don't want to go with them."

"Maybe they're both fatsos," my sister whispered, as she started to giggle.

Since my mom first fired the bullets into our wall and until the men in the white coats arrived, we had not exited our room. In fact, we had not even gotten up off the mattress.

As we continued to play the game, we hoped and prayed to Baby Jesus that this would finally be the horrific act that would cause one of our uncles or our grandparents to ride to the rescue and deliver us to a loving, permanent home—a home filled with food, lights, heat, and clean, unripped clothes, and devoid of dysfunctional and destructive adults.

In our grim and cemented reality, however, hopes, dreams, and prayers never were realized. No one came to our rescue. No one even knew.

Each day we remained unrescued made me wonder if we were worth saving.

Even though we could flat-out not believe it, our mom—the woman who had fired multiple bullets at us—was released from the loony bin and sent back to codirecting our mental and physical torture, before "two shakes of a lamb's tail," as she was fond of saying.

Wow.

14

A Gift Makes a Difference

Earlier that same year, I was given something that helped to change and form my young life in a very positive way. I was given an inexpensive telescope.

While far from the best, at my age and at that chaotic time, it was the best present in the world. Just the best. Thanks to it—or more precisely thanks to my Papa McNeil, who gave it to me—my interest in space and science grew exponentially. I was hooked. Until it was lost in a move a few months later, I spent every single clear night looking through that telescope at the stars and the moon and dreaming of being among them. Every night.

Thanks to that white cardboard tube, my love of science only grew. By the time I was ten, just as the mad scientist in me was beginning to sprout, our nomadic existence found us living in New Boston, New Hampshire. Certifiably crazy mother and all.

It was in New Boston that I really began to translate my growing interest in all things science into various projects and experiments. One of the first things I did was teach myself how to make my own gunpowder. *Real* gunpowder. After a few trips to the local drugstore and a nearby coal bin, I was soon making buckets of the stuff.

I was making the gunpowder for only *one* reason. I wanted to build a rocket to launch myself into space. Spaceflight was my ultimate dream, and I was trying to make it come real all by myself. In fact, I was consumed with the idea. Who needed NASA when I could build my own rockets?

But my little enterprise soon got me into big trouble, all because I didn't keep my discovery to myself. I decided to share my "genius" with my brother. He in turn, shared it with some of his lowlife friends in New Boston. Bad idea.

Aside from trying to build rockets with my gunpowder, I branched out and also made my own sticks of explosives. Again, *real* explosives. Actually, each one was about the size of a quarter stick of dynamite, and they produced a very powerful and very loud *boom*.

After my brother told them, his friends came around asking if they could have some samples. "Have?" No way. "Buy?" Sure. I was always looking for ways to make some money for the family. Worse idea.

It turns out, these "friends" of my brother used my dynamite to try to blow open the door of the local general store and got caught. Idiots.

Once caught, I guess it took them two seconds to rat me out as the seller and manufacturer of the dynamite. While bad news for me, there was a silver lining.

These older kids were caught by the chief of police for New Boston. I happened to be friends with the chief's incredibly nice daughter, Debbie, as we both had crushes on each other at the time. So, because of that and because I was only ten years old, I got off with a warning, while pretending to give him all the gunpowder I had left.

There was no way I was giving up on my dream to get into

space, and to get there, I needed fuel. That gunpowder was still going to be the fuel.

New Boston was actually mostly good memories for me. Even though we only lived there nine months, we managed to fit in at the public school and with the town. Even me.

On the other hand, New Boston is not as great a memory for my sister, Janice, who was now seven. The main reason? Me and some temporary insanity caused by any one of the zillion issues pounding us.

It was the middle of winter, and the night before, the mad scientist in me had taken an empty half-gallon milk container, filled it with water, and left it out on the deck to freeze. No doubt I was conducting one of my many experiments of the time and, for some reason, needed to freeze the water.

Well, the next morning when I went out on the deck to check its progress, I noticed that it was indeed frozen solid. I also noticed something else. My little sister was about ten feet below the deck making snow angels on the ground. How cute.

To this day, I have no rational or even irrational explanation for what I did next. Most likely trying to replicate the work of Sir Isaac Newton while settling a score with my sister for some previous slight.

As my tiny little sister Janice stood up in the snow to prepare to make her next snow angel, I picked up the heavy frozen block of ice covered in wax paper and held it—more or less—over her head. Like the bombardier in a B-52, just when I thought she was in range, I released my bomb load. Fortunately for her—and me—at the last second, my target moved.

So . . . instead of the block of ice smashing onto the top of her head, it glanced off her right ear and thumped onto her right shoulder. Janice went down like a sack of potatoes. Unfortunately, once crumpled on the snow, she did something a sack of potatoes wouldn't do. She started screaming bloody murder.

As I took off running toward a field across the street, I noticed the last snow angel I had *helped* her make. It didn't look nearly as neat as the others. Where was the dedication to her art?

15

The Caped Crusader Saves Our Lives

Per the norm, we were eventually evicted from our nice home in New Boston to a "new" home that looked like something from the TV show *Dark Shadows*. One night while living in that new home, my mom had to go get my dad, who was too drunk to drive home. She wanted the three of us to go with her, but we refused.

She kept insisting, and as the unofficial—and most likely self-elected—spokesperson for my brother and sister, I kept saying no. I had good reasons for my stubbornness.

For starters, it was the first time in weeks that we had electricity. Second, because we had electricity, it was also the first time in weeks we were able to watch the small black-and-white TV in the kitchen. Third, we were watching *Batman*.

The last and most important reason we didn't want to go with my mom was that we simply didn't want to be subjected, once again, to a smelly, filthy bar and have our dad humiliate us as he stumbled out toward the car. So, for all those reasons, I stood my ground.

We were going to finish watching *Batman* and that was that.

. . .

Neither my mom nor dad came home that night. The next morning, we got a call from my grandparents saying that my mom had been in a terrible car accident and was in the hospital. It was touch-and-go whether she would make it through the next few days.

The car had been totaled beyond recognition, and if we had been with her, we would not have survived. Thank you, electricity, Adam West, Julie Newmar (I was *really* in love with her), and stubborn pride.

We were living in Rat-Hole, Connecticut, and my grandparents said that my uncle Neil and aunt Barbara were coming down from Norwood, Massachusetts, to pick us up so we could live with them for a while.

Neil was one of my father's younger brothers and just an incredible uncle. He and Aunt Barbara took us into their warm and loving home, and in a very real sense, changed our lives in a positive way forever. Mine especially.

We only spent two months with them, but it was the two best months of our entire childhoods. We had normalcy. Not for just a day or a weekend like at our grandparents', but for weeks on end. For the first time in our lives, we went to a new school clean, wearing new clothes, and feeling welcomed by the other kids. For the first time in our young lives, we were not targets to be humiliated and ignored.

This act of generosity and kindness came at a trying time for Uncle Neil and Aunt Barbara. They had just recently welcomed their first child, David, into their lives. And about two weeks before we had shown up, David had, at about eight months of age, broken his leg.

And yet, with all of that going on, they still took us into their home as if we were their own children. At least for me, that serves as the main reason I fought so hard for "normalcy" in my life. Uncle Neil and Aunt Barbara showed me that our life was anything but normal and that there was a better way. From that moment on, I was determined to find it.

Of course, that's not to say that I wasn't a bit of a handful for my aunt Barbara. For her, it must have seemed that a completely wild baby wolverine had just entered her peaceful home and life. But even though I was somewhat difficult and strong-willed—my Uncle Peter later told me I was "the most ornery, stubborn little bastard" he had ever known—Aunt Barbara was more than up to the challenge. *Seriously* up to the challenge.

When my mom got "better" and we were once again forced to go back to her and my dad, my sister and I cried ourselves to sleep every night for a long time. Why would the relatives who said they loved us throw us back into the nightmare that was our lives? *Why?*

I had a *very* tough time doing the math on that one. Surely all of my adult relatives knew of our horrible and destructive existence. Why would they make us go back to *that?* Why would they purposely send us back into years of more suffering? Didn't they love us? Didn't they understand? Didn't they care?

Care, they did. In more ways than I would ever know.

Uncle Peter later informed me that Aunt Barbara and Uncle Neil wanted to legally adopt us and bring us into their home. *Permanently.*

He said it never happened because my mom had screamed the most hurtful things at Aunt Barbara, as she struck out in a rage at the thought of another woman raising us. Because of that outburst and my mom's threatened but phony legal actions, the adoption was stopped in its tracks, and our life sentence was extended.

My mom's misplaced and despicable conduct aside, the fact that two such wonderful people cared about us enough to even contemplate such a move gave me a burst of pride and joy.

16

Shining Shoes, Darts, and the She-Beast

Our next move was back to Dorchester. We actually moved to Hamilton Street, where our grandparents lived. Better than that, we moved directly across the street from them. For as long as it lasted, Janice, Jay, and I had an escape hatch thirty seconds away.

Along with that move came my first paying job as a shoe-shine boy. I was eleven and was shining shoes at a car dealership called Robie Ford. This particular car dealership was about three blocks from our apartment at 16 Hamilton Street.

It was thanks to my best friend, Gerry Donovan, that I got the job. Gerry was two years younger than me and had already been shining shoes there for more than six months.

I had actually met Gerry a few years earlier when we were staying at our grandparents' for the weekend. I remember sitting in my grandmother's living room watching *Daniel Boone* when the front door sprang open and a little tornado of a kid flew through and jumped up on the sofa next to me.

This kid looked up at me and said, "Hi, my name is Gerry. I live across the street. What are we watching?"

A few years after that introduction, I came to understand that Gerry had been created in the Petri dish of entrepreneurship, and by the time he was nine, was starting to frame his career.

While Gerry used the money he made shining shoes for movie

tickets, toys, candy, and normal "kid" things, I gave the few dollars I made every day after school and on weekends to my mom so she could buy food for our family. Little did I know that most if not all of the money I made was used to buy vodka for her and my father.

Ironically, even though I shined the very nice shoes of the car salesmen and their customers, I went out of my way to make sure they never got a good look at the shoes on my own feet.

My shoes had gotten so bad that the sole of my right shoe was completely unattached, so that every time I walked, it would make a loud flapping noise.

Because my shoe was now noticeably flapping, kids in school and the neighborhood were once again starting to make fun of me. I went to my mom and dad and begged for a new pair of shoes so the kids wouldn't pick on me. They looked down at me, smiled with booze-altered grins, and shook their heads no. They told me that they had no money for shoes, and yet that very night, my dad came home from the package store with two huge bottles of vodka.

In desperation not to have the kids in school, or even my friends, taunt me anymore, I cut what was left of the sole off the bottom of my right shoe. By doing this, I of course exposed the bottom of my right foot to the street, dirt, rocks, and glass.

Within days, the bottom of my right foot was sliced open and bleeding nonstop from numerous small cuts. To offer my foot some protection, I learned to wrap part of a newspaper around my foot and then tape it in place. In my mind, all of that was a small price to pay in order not to have kids make fun of me.

The time we lived at 16 Hamilton Street was a bit of a family record. We stayed there almost twelve months before being evicted. Twelve months was like a lifetime for my brother, sister, and me.

Because we lived there longer than we lived at most other

places, we managed to accumulate a few warm, funny, and bizarre memories.

The best and most enduring memory was that anytime we needed a hug or to feel loved, we simply had to walk across the street and be greeted by our grandparents, who, as always, would smother us with love, affection, and a square meal.

I also remember that address for a very emotional reason. It was at 16 Hamilton Street that we had our one and *only* "normal" Christmas.

My dad had actually been sober for a few months—also a record—and was making regular money doing something nobody wanted to know anything about and was able to buy my brother, sister, and me a few presents from the five-and-dime store up on Bowdoin Street. Of course, since most Christmases we got no presents and often had no tree, this was an amazing treat for us.

We also got to sit down for a real Christmas dinner as a family. The first and last time that ever happened as well.

By the time of this first and only normal Christmas, I understood that I did not think or act like most children. I was forever immersed in my own world, my own thoughts, and my own dreams.

As such, I loved Christmas for what it meant to me. The birthday of Baby Jesus. To me, Christmas was a time to be grateful, a time to be reflective, and a time to share.

CBS was showing a special that year called *A Charlie Brown Christmas*. The "meaning of Christmas" speech by Linus spoke louder than any sermon in any church. It stuck with me when little else did.

During that wonderful program, when Charlie Brown cries out in desperation, "Isn't there anyone who knows what Christmas is all about?" Linus responds from a platform of pure and simple faith: "Sure, Charlie Brown, I can tell you what Christmas is all about."

Linus then steps to the center of the stage and recites from Luke's gospel (2:8–14):

And there were in the same country shepherds abiding in the field, keeping watch over their flock by night. And, lo, the angel of the Lord came upon them, and the glory of the Lord shone round about them: and they were sore afraid. And the angel said unto them, Fear not: for, behold, I bring you good tidings of great joy, which shall be to all people. For unto you is born this day in the city of David a Savior, which is Christ the Lord. And this shall be a sign unto you; Ye shall find the babe wrapped in swaddling clothes, lying in a manger. And suddenly there was with the angel a multitude of the heavenly host praising God, and saying, Glory to God in the highest, and on earth peace, good will toward men.

For me, that was the true and *only* meaning of Christmas. Weirdly, because of that belief and despite the fact that we lived in abject poverty, I had more empathy and sympathy than was good for me.

I remember that during this one "special" Christmas, a young boy about my age came to our front door collecting for some kind of charity. It was an especially cold winter in Boston, and this young boy had no coat on and was shivering quite badly. My empathy alarm started to sound, and I immediately went to get the money I had been hiding away so I could buy myself a cheap baseball glove. I grabbed those few dollars from their secret hiding place and gave them to this small, shivering boy with no coat.

Of course, a few months later, I saw him again on the streets of Dorchester and followed him a few blocks to see how much worse he had it than me. *Surprise.* He ended up walking into one of the most luxurious homes in the whole neighborhood. It turned out that his family had a great deal of money, and he just didn't like to wear a coat.

Even though I found out he wasn't poor, I still hoped the money I gave him for the charity was now helping other poor children. I was a baby bird with two broken wings looking to save baby birds with one or no broken wings.

I think my brother, Jay, bought the first set of darts in our neighborhood, and then all of a sudden all our friends went down to Mike's—the corner store on Hamilton Street—and bought their own.

The second best part about living at 16 Hamilton Street—after having my grandparents across the street—was that my very best friend, Gerry Donovan, lived up on the third floor. Sixteen Hamilton Street was a "triple-decker." We lived on the first floor, the landlord lived on the second floor, and Gerry and his family lived on the third.

The Donovans were and are a wonderful family. Like most people back then, Gerry's mom and dad were dealing with a few issues—issues that, to their great credit, they eventually overcame.

Gerry was the oldest child in the family, followed by Maureen, Virginia, Carol, and Charlie. Gerry was *my* best friend, and Maureen was my sister's best friend. That made life a little more enjoyable for a short period of time.

Even as a small kid, Gerry was a rock, and more important, he had my back. And because we were the two most hated and hunted kids in that section of Dorchester, protecting each other became a full-time job.

As said, Gerry was a businessman at birth. All this guy ever wanted to do was figure out a way to get ahead. But balancing that very healthy ambition was a great deal of spirituality and faith.

Gerry and I hung out with some good kids and some not-so-good kids. But mostly we hung out with each other. In a world of "experimentation" and petty and not-so-petty crime, neither one of us ever smoked, drank, or did drugs. Not ever. Not once.

We may have done some crazy things, but we did them with all of our faculties intact.

In Gerry I was also fortunate enough to find a mirror image of myself, in the sense that Gerry was fascinated by the world and business and wanted more out of life than hanging out on the local street corner with kids who were going nowhere.

To speak to Gerry's maturity and certitude of direction: by the time he was twenty-three he was married and had two children, a successful business, and a beautiful home in the suburbs of Boston. By anyone's definition, Gerry Donovan had become a true success and a pillar of his community.

But that success story wasn't *quite* the Gerry Donovan I knew when we had real darts to play with.

One of the older kids—to a twelve-year-old, two or three years older than you was *really* old—convinced Gerry to do something awe-inspiringly stupid. Stupid as in it makes you sit bolt upright in bed thirty years later drenched in a cold sweat asking yourself, "What the heck was I thinking!?" *That* kind of stupid.

This older kid, whose name was Frederick, had taken a plastic orange from his mom's fruit basket. Don't ask me how, but he somehow convinced Gerry to play William Tell. Except in this case, instead of arrows flying at Gerry's head, it would be steel-tipped darts thrown by unbalanced, zit-sporting teenagers with me as an audience.

Once Gerry innocently agreed to this stark-raving-crazy game, I, Gerry, Frederick, my brother Jay, and our other older friend Mickey walked behind the garage at 16 Hamilton Street to commence the madness.

In retrospect, I, as Gerry's best friend and the one who was supposed to have his back, should have spoken up. But at twelve, I foolishly thought the older guys knew what they were doing and no harm would come to Gerry. Whoops.

Frederick positioned Gerry—who was about ten at the time—with his back against the garage wall. Frederick and the rest of us then walked about fifteen feet away from the still-smiling, eager-to-please Gerry.

I think because he—like me—was so young and trusting of an older kid, Gerry did not look at all nervous standing against the garage wall with a plastic orange as a target sitting on top of his thick brown head of hair. Not the least bit nervous.

Being Gerry's best friend, I knew something about him the other kids didn't. Gerry had a seriously bad temper. Al Capone bad.

I prayed it was a temper we would not see in action in a few seconds. But it was a prayer that went unanswered.

I suspect that some of the angels in Heaven took a break from saving souls and fluffing clouds to watch the impending explosion.

Once he had Gerry positioned against the wall, Frederick walked back next to us. With the red, steel-tipped dart in his right hand, Frederick proceeded to wind up like a steroid-juiced major-league pitcher. He threw—or *whipped* as we said back then—the first dart in Gerry's direction. He whipped it so hard that we couldn't see it in flight. We mostly just heard the *whooosssssshhh* and turned our heads toward Gerry.

Frederick not only missed the plastic orange still sitting neatly on top of Gerry's head, but he missed *Gerry* completely. The red dart had buried itself into the gray garage wall about five feet to Gerry's right. That wasn't a good sign.

Fortunately, with Frederick's next throw, he seemed to find his range. Well, almost. The second dart landed smack in the middle of Gerry's forehead.

At first, for at least a nanosecond, there was complete silence. Even the birds, rats, and squirrels stopped what they were doing to watch. The four of us were shocked into silence by what had just happened. Gerry was totally silent because there was a good chance he was dead or in a coma.

But about a second later, that proved not to be the case. Gerry went absolutely berserk. Completely nuts. He was crying and screaming so hard that spittle and snot were flying everywhere.

Had he stood there a few more seconds, he would have repainted the wall of the garage.

But he did not stay. Gerry yanked the dart out of the middle of his forehead and charged at Frederick. Frederick ran like a bat out of hell, but it turned out he was a very slow bat.

Even at ten, Gerry was strong. He was a good Little League player and had a really strong right arm. Just as Frederick was about to disappear over the hill at the top of Hamilton Street, Gerry threw the now-bloodied dart with all of his might, anger, and snot.

The dart hit Frederick right in the middle of his spine. It may sound cruel now, but all of us, even Gerry, laughed our butts off at the sight of Frederick running screaming into his apartment, trying unsuccessfully to pull the red dart out of the middle of his back.

That was one of the few funny memories I have of our time at 16 Hamilton Street. The inverse of that was a bizarre moment when Jay and I were coming home early from the snob-infested Gate of Heaven Catholic high school in South Boston.

If I may, I'd like to digress a moment and explain why I thought Gate of Heaven was such a terrible place. Before being forced into that school, I was happily going to a poor-ish public school in Dorchester—Grover Cleveland Junior High School.

Unfortunately for me, my brother—who was also going to Grover Cleveland Junior High—had decided that he really needed and wanted to go to Gate of Heaven. Unlike me, he really liked parochial schools. That was one reason. The other reason was that he *really* needed to get out of Grover Cleveland—immediately.

While attending our very tough public junior high school, Jay—and I have his permission to tell this story—had his ass kicked by a girl.

Every day at Grover Cleveland when school let out, you only

had to walk about ten feet before you found a couple hundred kids in a circle watching some junior gladiator match. Most of the time, I just ignored them as I wanted to go home and practice picking locks or drawing up plans to rob the Museum of Fine Arts.

But on this particular day, the crowd of kids watching the fight was at least twice as large as a normal fight crowd. Possibly, I thought, the two toughest kids in the school were finally going at it. That would be the two guys we referred to as "Cro-Magnon" and "Ice Age." They each had one thick, continuous eyebrow above both their eyes and a hairline that started just above the fur eyebrow, were about six foot five, weighed about three hundred pounds, and were most likely forty years old in the eighth grade. They were beyond prehistoric.

As I fought my way to the front of the fight crowd in eager anticipation of seeing Ice Age and Cro-Magnon duke it out for the undisputed title of the netherworld, I slowed when I spotted what looked like Jay's shirt and pants rolling around on the ground.

No way four hundred kids are going to stop to watch my brother in a fight. Fighting was just not Jay's thing. One of the times we moved back to Dorchester from New Hampshire, Jay decided that the only way to fight was to fight *clean*.

His new rule was soon put to the test. A few weeks earlier, Jay was fighting some total slimeball from Mt. Everett Street. He actually had this very tough kid on the ground when he instituted his new "rule." He let the kid up because that was the "fair" thing to do. Just as he was doing that, I screamed, "Knife!"

Well, I was wrong. It was actually a razor. In one move, the thug sliced my brother's tie right off his body. Jay then did something very smart. He sprinted all the way home. He may have set a new world record, but none of us had a stopwatch at the time.

Clearly, Jay was not a fighter. Even so, it sure looked like his clothes getting their ass kicked in the street next to Grover Cleveland. As I finally pushed my way to the front of the circle, my worst fear was confirmed, and Jay's nightmare was beginning.

It was my brother fighting, and *losing* to, a girl. A very, very big girl with a mustache and a deep voice, but until DNA testing proves otherwise, still some kind of female humanoid.

Normally I would have jumped in and tried to save him. This time, however, I turned on one heel and took off as fast as I could. Not because I didn't want to save him from this whupping at the hands, feet, and teeth of the Daughter of the Hulk, but rather because I didn't want him to know that his little brother had just seen him losing to a Tasmanian devil in a dress.

I shouldn't have worried. It was *the* story at school the next day. I think it was also front page, above the fold, in the *Boston Globe* sports section.

So for that reason, and a few others, Jay thought it best to be at Gate of Heaven. I should never have gone with him.

Gate of Heaven in South Boston was by no means a wealthy school. Middle class at best. But even at that, we were still the poorest kids in school. And it was only a matter of days before some of the kids started torturing me because of my poverty. You would think it would stop when you entered high school, but it only got worse.

Strangely enough, the girls were often crueler than the boys. One girl in particular.

It just so happened, she was the girl I had a serious crush on. Her name was Anne and she was Filipino-American and because her last name also began with *M,* she sat in front of me in most classes.

At first she really seemed to like me, and several of her friends told me that she had a crush on me. That lasted about a week or so, until it dawned on her and her equally superficial friends that I had worn the same ripped pants; dirty, unironed shirt; tie; and sport coat to school over and over.

As the most popular girl in class, she couldn't have the other kids thinking that she actually liked me, so from that moment on she and her friends began to tear me down. Her insults lasted right up to the moment I managed to escape that asylum. My only crime, once again, was that I was beyond poor.

What Anne and her fellow tormentors did not know—or worse and more likely, did not care about—was that I simply didn't know better. At thirteen I still had not been equipped with the tools or the means to make myself more presentable in public. Whatever spare time I did have was spent trying to figure out how to feed and look after my brother, sister, and me.

Consequently, I didn't know how to take care of myself. I didn't get to bathe properly. I didn't have a dentist. I didn't have . . . period. *That* was my crime.

Her crime was that she was ignorant and insecure. Sadly, she made me pay the price for her failings.

For that reason and more, I really detested that school and the kids who made going after me a sport.

One afternoon while Jay and I were coming home early from that awful school, we got the most vivid example of the extreme measures a landlord might take after being cheated out of rent money by our father.

It was a warm, sunny May day. Jay and I had gotten off the bus at Columbia Road and were just walking up Hamilton Street when we noticed two Boston police cars parked in front of our triple-decker. Big deal. We were more than used to seeing police cars in front of our homes. Even so, we were somewhat surprised to see them because things had been mostly quiet between our parents. When we got closer, we found out why the police were needed.

Well, in a fit of rage at not being paid, "Mrs. G"—our landlord, who would make a crackhead on her worst day look normal—

took a broom handle and systematically smashed every single window in our apartment.

We were told later that she did all this wearing a very short, very revealing nightgown. You had to at least give her points for style if not for brains. I think the police let her change out of her nightgown and into regular clothes before they hauled her off to be booked.

17

The Broken Bunch

When we did have electricity, I watched a few episodes of a new show called *The Brady Bunch*. When I did, I thought Greg, Marcia, Jan, and the rest of the cast on the show were aliens from another planet. *Nobody* human lived like that. No children really lived in a house that nice or with that much love. It was just not possible.

Where was the squalor that was my life? Where was the twisted and disturbing reality of our mostly decaying homes and always temporary neighborhoods?

For Janice, Jay, and I, *The Brady Bunch, The Partridge Family,* and all the other "happy family" shows on the air only served to remind us how truly painful, pathetic, and dangerous our young lives really were. Instead of worrying if we had the latest and coolest style of clothes to wear for the first day of school—like Keith, Greg, Marcia, or Laurie—we had to fear how much the other kids were going to torment us for the old, dirty, or ripped clothes we wore, or the smell that came from our unwashed bodies and garments.

For many kids, back-to-school is an exciting time. A new year with new friends and new possibilities. Most of our schoolmates lacked for nothing as they reentered school, styling the latest fashions and gadgets of the time. For me, Jay, and Janice, the first day of school was fraught with embarrassment, humiliation, envy, and outright depression.

For us, the first day of school meant possibly running a gauntlet of teasing or outright cruelty, and for reasons beyond our control. We had done nothing wrong but had to pay a severe price, with lasting effects, for the neglect of our parents.

We dreaded that first day not only because almost everyone would be parading in their shiny new clothes, but because more than a few would be looking for those less fortunate. Looking for someone to bully and destroy.

For us, when the back-to-school commercials hit the airwaves, we became more than depressed. We became afraid.

Even at that age, I knew we were far from the only children going through this embarrassment and pain. Because of our circumstances, we often lived in some very poor places with some other very poor children. I also knew that the poorer the school, the less chance we had of being picked on. But even at that, when the finger-pointing and taunting did start, I still felt very much alone.

When I very reluctantly and very slowly walked to school the first day of the new school year, I wondered if anyone really cared about kids like us. Did anyone give us a second thought?

Why should they? For most people, we were an invisible class of children who rarely, if ever, entered their very comfortable lives. How could they think about us if we didn't exist? And if we didn't exist, then we needed no help.

I knew that we—like the other faceless and nameless poor children in the country and the world—had nothing simply because we were born. Born into the wrong neighborhood, born to the wrong parents or parent, or born into tragic circumstances. And because we were born, sooner or later we had to deal with those first days of school. The first days without. The first days of being ripped apart because of something totally beyond our control.

We were born.

18

Insane Friends and Armed Robbery

When not in school but still in those old and dirty clothes, and on those often dangerous streets, I never had to look for trouble or crime. It found me.

And when it did, I had to make a decision. Usually right on the spot.

While it would be nice to say that my first thought when this trouble descended upon me was *What would Jesus do?* that wasn't the case.

While I did in fact use that question as a regular test for many dilemmas, when someone was about to cave in my face or slam a piece of sharp steel into me, the actual real first questions to enter my mind were usually *How did I get myself into this mess?* and *How do I make it out alive?*

There are two sides to every crime—the perpetrator's and the victim's—and I found myself on both sides on a number of occasions. Sometimes I was the willing perpetrator . . . sometimes the victim . . . and on a few occasions, I was swept along with the friends I chose to keep. All in all, I was proud of myself for not falling into the dark side of poverty.

The "dark" side was inhabited by those who said they used drugs, mugged people, or did much worse because of poverty and because "nobody cared about them." Give me a break.

That lame rationale was just an excuse, and a very dishonest one at that. They used drugs, robbed people, or did worse because they were weak, had no morals, were beyond lazy, and were looking to score money or instant gratification the easiest way possible. Nothing more complicated than that.

Simple and so much easier than hard work. But I could never go there. Because of the pain that I and my family went through every day, I couldn't stand to see others in pain. My empathy and belief in the Golden Rule were honed at the very heights of dysfunction.

So even at twelve and thirteen, I knew that if I robbed someone, they would be in a large degree of pain. Either physically or emotionally, or both. I did not want to be the cause of such fear and anguish. Ever.

Nor did I want to steal. Because *we* had nothing, I knew that if I stole from others, my crime would cause them additional pain and add more of a burden to their already complicated lives. I know that sounds a little deep for a thirteen-year-old, but I was a strange kid.

Unlike Robin Hood and his band of "merry" men, who only robbed from the rich to give to the poor, some of the guys I knew only robbed from the poor to give to the poorer . . . themselves. No trickle-down economics here. Mostly just pee trickling down the leg of whoever was being held up at the moment.

As much as I and my best friend, Gerry, tried to avoid crime and hurting others, sometimes the friends we hung out with didn't quite see it that way.

One particular "friend" of mine could have landed both of us in juvenile detention or even adult prison. This kid was *way* north of insane, with an appointment with a SWAT team and prison food booked at birth.

Ben and I were walking through Prudential Center in downtown Boston on a tranquil Sunday afternoon. I'm guessing that Ben was about fourteen at the time, with me thirteen.

As we were walking—again, at two o'clock in the afternoon, in broad daylight, with all kinds of people in our general area—an older couple was walking toward us. Since it was a Sunday, both the man and the woman were very well dressed. He was wearing a suit and tie, and she was wearing a very elegant dress.

As I took a quick look at them, I guessed they were about the age of my grandparents. Of course, when you are thirteen years old, anyone older seems ancient.

As Ben and I closed the distance between them, we were talking about nothing. Just talking smack. Whatever. Most certainly we were not talking about doing anything bad. At least Ben and I weren't. Ben and his twisted mind were apparently having a very loud and animated conversation between themselves, to which I was not privy.

As the older couple smiled at us and was just walking by, and while I was in midsentence telling Ben about how my Red Sox "hero" Carl Yastrzemski once dragged me down the street with my hand stuck in the door handle of his car just because I was trying to get an autograph, Ben pulled out a switchblade and held it to the throat of the old man. Uh-oh.

What happened next was a blur as my mind slowed to a crawl from outright disbelief.

"Give me your f---ing wallet, old man, an' no one gets hurt," hissed Ben in the guy's ear.

At that moment, I was sure of three things: First, Ben's very fragile mind had finally snapped. Second, I was about to go to prison for something I didn't do or know was about to happen. And third, if I survived all this, my "friendship" with Ben was definitely over.

Like many, many truly poor people, I had been scared or nervous most of my young life. Not scared or afraid of bad things or bad people in the street, but more afraid of the unexpected.

For that and many reasons, I hated to see innocent people scared. I really hated it. Seeing the fear in this couple's face as Ben held a knife to the throat of the husband made me sad beyond comprehension. Life is hard enough without sudden and terrifying fear being added to the list.

It also made me instantly angry.

"What are you *doing?*" I screamed at Ben.

He kept the knife at the old man's throat and looked at me. "Shut up, man. I'm making us some money."

I grabbed his arm and forced it away from the old man's throat. "Sorry, sorry, sorry," I said to the couple. "He was just kidding. Just his idea of a joke."

Before Ben could reengage, the couple had the sense to scurry on their way. As they did, I remember saying over and over again, "I'm so sorry, I'm so sorry, I'm so sorry," as I instinctively swiveled my head back and forth looking for the police or witnesses.

Upon seeing none, I let loose on Ben with every curse word I could think of before taking off at full speed in the opposite direction of the elderly couple, who were sure to flag down the cops at any second.

As for the deranged Ben, I never saw him again after that Sunday afternoon.

During this time, I never stole anything or stole from anybody. Never . . . unless you count a few hundred pens and pencils.

That is not to say that I was an angel. Far from it. My thing back then was trying to be more clever than the adults. If I couldn't be an astronaut, then I wanted to be a master criminal and jewel thief—just like Alexander Mundy on my favorite TV show, *It Takes a Thief.*

Consequently, what I did do back then, and became very, very good at, was picking locks and breaking into places. I also became quite good at picking pockets. So much so that in the seventh and eighth grades at Grover Cleveland Junior High School in Dorchester, I created my own business.

I picked the pockets of almost every kid in school. What I picked was their pens and pencils, which I would then sell back to them for five cents apiece. I am not proud of those petty crimes. Even though I used the little bit of money I made to help my family, it was still wrong. Amazingly, no one ever suspected a thing, and it was a lucrative business right up until the point that I transferred to the "Gate of Superficial Kids" high school.

I also gained the reputation for being able to open combination padlocks as well as combination lockers. It actually got to the point where the school would page me over the intercom to come pick some kid's locker because he and the school couldn't get into it.

So while I never stole anything except pens and pencils from anybody, that is not to say that I did not commit crimes. I committed many of them. What I did was called "breaking and entering," and it was a real and punishable crime. Luckily for me, I never came close to getting caught.

I broke into countless homes, businesses, and stores. I always picked the locks or defeated the alarm systems on the windows and did it for the personal satisfaction I got from the accomplishment.

I wanted to beat the system. More important, I *needed* to beat the system. Why? Maybe like the man who walks deep into a forest and screams as loud as he can to prove to himself that he's still alive and kicking, I had to make some kind of mark. Even if said mark was reckless and could have landed me in juvenile detention or worse.

What I did, while wrong, truly were harmless crimes inasmuch as I never took anything and no one ever knew I had entered, much less left, their premises.

I thought I deserved at least a few style points for the smoothness of it all.

• • •

One of my proudest moments as a kid criminal came when I picked the lock of the control tower at Logan International Airport in Boston. Thus I was able to sneak all over the control tower of a major airport and the employees never knew I was there.

Not bad for a thirteen-year-old punk.

The reason I was at the airport in the first place was that it was one of my hiding places from the pain at home. Every chance I got, once I collected a quarter or so, I would take the T—the Boston subway system—to the airport and hang out all day watching the planes land and take off. I would do this on weekends and even the occasional weekday, when something truly traumatic happened at home and my mind needed the respite of aircraft over teachers.

I had hung out at the airport so many times that a few of the pilots and stewardesses were actually kind enough to talk to me and even show me around a few of the aircraft. Usually, after the tour, they would figure out a way to buy me a hamburger while doing that shaking of their heads thing off to the side.

There were a number of pilots and stewardesses who took pity on me, but I especially remember the kindness of those who worked for the old Eastern Air Lines. Not only did they show me a few of the planes, but they also answered my endless questions and loaded me up with pins, Eastern Air Line ticket jackets, and small replicas of the Lockheed Constellation—my favorite aircraft of all time—and the Lockheed Electra.

The kindness of strangers became the ingredients for escape and "success."

19

The Wrong Side of Crime
and Attempted Murder

I was also on occasion—and always in Dorchester—on the receiving side of violent crime. Aside from getting stabbed, a couple of other incidents made a lasting impression as well.

The first was when Gerry and I were walking back from the local drugstore down on Columbia Road, where we would buy soda and candy. We were just minding our own business talking about our sad Little League team, which was actually managed by my beloved uncle Tom.

This particular Little League team made the Bad News Bears look like the Boston Red Sox by comparison. We were bad, we were strange, and we really didn't fit in. Our team was mostly composed—and I certainly include myself in this description—of miniature versions of the creatures you'd see in any bad horror flick playing at the local drive-in. Few teams wanted to play us. Either because of our smell, our look, or a general fear that we might morph into zombies at any second and start to look at them as if they were giant hot dogs.

Uncle Tom more than had his hands full with that team.

As Gerry and I were shuffling along the street, we wondered

aloud which hard-ass in the area might be harboring a grudge against us at that particular moment. No matter the day, there was always someone who thought he had to settle a score with us.

As it turned out, we didn't have to wait long to get the answer to that daily question. A few seconds after turning the corner onto Hamilton Street, the passenger window of the car parked next to us exploded into a million pieces.

Gerry and I might not have been the two smartest kids on the planet, but we had doctorates in street smarts. We may not have known what was going on, but we knew that an exploding car window was not normal. Both of us instantly hit the sidewalk as we tried to figure out what was happening.

The answer came about one second later as another window of the car exploded in a shower of glass. This time we heard the gunshot that came with the explosion. Another normal day in the lives of "Gerry and Doug." Someone else was trying to kill us. Get in line, moron.

Without going into the sordid details, Gerry and I were basically a two-man gang and had pretty much alienated every thug in the neighborhood. And I mean *all* of them.

Guns, knives, bullets, pipes, bricks, rocks, two-by-fours, whatever. Most of them had come our way at one point or another.

After the second gunshot, there was no detective work needed to figure out who was doing the shooting. That was because the shooter started screaming at Gerry and me from his perch across the street and removed all of the guesswork.

"Hey, maggots"—he used much more vulgar language—"how do you like that? That's the last time you'll ever say shit about my sister again."

Okay. This particular drop-case who was shooting at us wasn't trying to scare us or send a message. He was truly trying to kill us.

Luckily, just as he was about to unload another round, the guy who owned the car, which was being turned into a colander, opened the window of his apartment right above our heads and started screaming like a madman. With that, the shooter took off running.

He ran, but Gerry and I both recognized the voice and dealt with him later. Nothing too serious, mind you. Just something to get the message across that we *really* didn't like to get shot at.

The message was clearly received, and he never bothered us again.

It turned out that the shooter had heard that Gerry and I were going around town telling kids his sister Lois was a little too friendly with the boys. Quite the opposite was true. At least for me. Lois was fourteen and one of the most beautiful girls I had ever seen. The last thing I was going to do was say anything negative about her. I wanted her to like me.

I never did find the courage to speak with her and tell her I thought she was wonderful. But the truth of how I felt about her didn't stop the destructive and dangerous misinformation from being spread. For most people, rumors or perceived insults are dealt with by employing constructive and honest dialogue. For the unhinged of the world—like the brother of Lois—you simply settle the matter by snapping off a few gunshots, in this case at two very young and innocent kids.

Soon after ducking those bullets, I found myself on the wrong end of a collection of fists and something much more lethal.

One night in the dark of winter, a group of these "humanoids" were having a lame party in the basement of a triple-decker on Mt. Everett Street. Mt. Everett Street was perpendicular to Hamilton Street and was the home of these burgeoning career criminals.

Once Gerry and I had heard about this party, we decided to peek in the basement window there and take a look. We also decided to bring along a few homemade "dart guns" we had crafted. Nothing bad. These dart guns just fired the erasers from the tops of pencils. Erasers that, not by coincidence, had common pins sticking out of the front. Along with the little dart guns we also brought broken paper clips to be fired from rubber bands.

During this same time period, I used to also build my own "zip guns," which were homemade guns that fired real bullets. I built a few of these, first to see if I could do it and second, to see if they would work. I could and they did. But I built them strictly for protection. Defensive weapons only and not in violation of the nonproliferation treaty.

Since no zip guns were called for on this particular assignment—I should have rethought that error in judgment—we were just intending to amuse ourselves with our little, mostly harmless, dart guns. The "darts," which were fired out of the equivalent of a large Slurpee straw, could travel quite far and actually stick into you, but they caused no real damage.

So . . . just two friends out to have a bit of harmless fun. What could go wrong?

Plenty, as it turned out. As these Enemies of the State of Doug and Gerry were dancing, drinking booze, and smoking pot in the basement of this triple-decker, Gerry and I amused ourselves to no end by firing these little darts and paper clips into their butts, necks, and the backs of their heads.

Either because most of them were wasted or because, as we always suspected, they were dumber than rocks, it took them a *very* long time to figure out what was happening to them. Gerry and I were almost wetting our pants from laughing ourselves silly at their cluelessness.

As we fired these darts, we could hear them say, "Ow. Something just stung me." Or "I think a spider just bit me." Or "Hey! Who just grabbed me?"

But as the adults say, it's fun until someone gets hurt. And that someone was about to become me. In a very big and violent way.

Gerry had just fired a dart into some girl's neck when she turned and looked right up at the basement window to see Gerry's and my faces illuminated by the lights in the basement.

The girl screamed to everyone in the party, "Look! It's those jerks from Hamilton Street!"

Hey, at least she knew who we were.

Now, as mentioned, there were a number of very large, very mean, and most likely very drunk or wasted thugs at that little party. At the sound of her scream, every one of those cave dwellers turned in unison, first to look at her and then to look at the still-laughing faces of Gerry and me in the window.

At that point, Gerry and I decided to run. For our lives.

These guys—or pincushions as they were now known—boiled out of the basement like a bunch of incredibly angry wasps. Psychotic wasps, actually.

Gerry and I made two mistakes that night. First, we grossly underestimated how many tough guys were at the party. And second, I forgot that our short-nightgown-wearing, broom-wielding landlord had just installed an eight-foot chain-link fence all around our triple-decker. Bad time to forget such an important detail.

As we were running and as about fifteen guys were chasing us, I decided to stop and fire the last dart I had left in the general direction of the posse. *Who* was stupid now?

As I was doing this, Gerry was over the fence like a monkey running from a pride of half-starved lions. I think he was in his bed and under the covers before the last dart flew from my straw. With his escape, he proved to be the much smarter of the two of us.

I fired the dart and *forgot*. I forgot about the fence.

Well . . . I forgot about it right until the second I bounced off it running full blast. That collision with the fence hurt quite a bit. The pain that followed made the pain of the fence seem like a long-lost relative with money.

No sooner did I bounce off this fence than the swarm of angry wasps was on me.

Because it was winter in Boston, there was a fair amount of snow on the ground. The snow made the darkness of night seem unusually bright. So bright that I could clearly see the snarling, almost drooling, faces of the fifteen or so guys.

Two of them picked me up off the ground—have I mentioned that most of these guys *really, really* hated me and Gerry for a variety of reasons?—and held me while the ringleader came over to me. Without saying a word, he smashed me on the right side of my face with his fist.

After that, I remember each of them taking a whack at me as they passed me around the circle. Even in my dazed condition, I knew this was probably not going to have a good ending.

At some point I fell to the ground and was lying there turning the snow around my head bright red with my blood. As I looked up, the ringleader was standing over me, now holding a very large rock. A rock he intended to drop on my head.

Just as he was lifting this boulder, a Boston police car came down the alley between the triple-deckers, with its siren going and blue light flashing. My only guess on this miraculous occurrence was that a neighbor had been looking out from a window and had called the cops. *Thank you.*

At the sight of the police car, the ringleader threw the boulder to the side, and he and his gang scattered like cockroaches when a kitchen light is flipped on.

While I had never been a fan of nosy neighbors, on this particular night I was thrilled that someone had called the police and that a patrol car had been in the neighborhood. The very definition of dumb luck.

There were, of course, many lessons to be learned from that experience, but the most important one for me was "Never forget when someone surrounds your property with an eight-foot chain-link fence."

It could be hazardous to your face, ribs, groin, nose, right eye, left big toe, Adam's apple, and several teeth. *Ouch.*

20

Don't Excuse the Inexcusable

All of this trauma, melodrama, and tumultuous extracurricular activity took place with almost no one but us combatants or participants being the wiser. Most certainly, without my mother and father knowing.

For most normal kids (although I guess most "normal" kids are never involved in these ill-considered situations), the logical thought process would be not to inform their mom and dad, so they wouldn't get in trouble. For me it was simply "Why waste my time?" Not only would they not care, but most likely they wouldn't even remember.

At twelve and thirteen years of age, I was already a huge believer in "need to know" and tended to play almost all information very close to the vest. Not only did I not inform my mom and dad of my questionable and hazardous activities, but I almost never told my brother, sister, or other friends. Why would I? I calculated and concluded well before twelve that there was little to be gained from such openness, but *much* to be lost.

I had already had it pounded into me that if you had a secret and then were trusting or stupid enough to tell that secret to someone else, human nature dictated that whoever you told would almost assuredly tell someone else. People love betraying secrets and, with them, whichever family member or friend told them the confidential information in the first place.

Having learned that invaluable lesson before I learned to ride a bike, I knew people couldn't tell what they didn't know.

Impenetrable compartmentalization was and is a good thing. Especially if the secret or simple truth could hurt you once in the hands of the wrong people. Topping that list of "wrong people" would be my mom and dad.

Between the two of them, my father most certainly met the definition of bad to very bad for most people—including numerous police departments across New England. My mom initially wasn't bad. Not in the strict sense of the word. In the beginning, she was ill-equipped and dysfunctional, and then she was beaten down to "bad."

Together they were the world champions of being feckless. My mom and dad were two highly dysfunctional people who had no business being together, and *seriously* had no business having children. They could not take care of themselves, let alone the three children they would bring into the world and proceed to ignore, deprive, and damage on a regular basis and on a number of levels.

As Jay, Janice, and I were ripped from place to place, constantly denied the basic necessities of life, while being humiliated every step of the way, various people, including my grandparents and uncles and aunts, tried to explain, excuse, or downplay the inexcusable behavior of my mom and dad.

No excuse or creative rationale offered up for my dad's criminal neglect could ever pass the smell test. For my mom, there was at least a hint of plausibility for excusing her irrational and uncaring behavior.

My mom's mom was herself a mess. She passed away from cirrhosis before any of us kids were born, but we grew to learn the facts. Two came into play: First, my grandmother on my mother's side was a severe alcoholic who also had a very abusive personality.

Second, apparently she was a generous woman. My grandmother was kind enough to pass those two traits along to her only child.

The complete opposite end of that parental spectrum was my mom's dad. George McNeil was a truly wonderful and elegant man and, as mentioned, was one of my few childhood heroes.

My mom's dad was a gifted, dignified person, and an incredibly talented golfer, who had a friendship with the great Francis Ouimet. As in the U.S. Open winner of 1913. As in the person who put U.S. golf on the map. As in the person the actor Shia LaBeouf portrayed in the Disney movie *The Greatest Game Ever Played.*

I can say without equivocation that during the times he visited or lived with us, he truly was my best real and human friend and strongest supporter. He was a wonderful and gentle soul.

Sadly for his grandchildren, he didn't pass enough of his DNA to his daughter.

Regarding my dad, I learned the truth about him at an incredibly early age: he could be an exceptionally bad person who did many things that bordered on evil.

Given that basic and unassailable truth, it was simply impossible to structure any kind of rationale for his conduct or the crimes he committed. Even worse, the crimes he committed against his own children.

My father came from an amazingly loving, normal, and accomplished family. His father—my Papa MacKinnon—was born in Nova Scotia and made his way down to Boston at a young age.

Once he had established himself in Boston, he had the great good fortune to meet a beautiful young woman by the name of Anna MacIssac. After courting—as they called it back then—they married, settled in Dorchester, had seven children, and were the bedrock of their community. They were an incredibly loving couple who didn't have a bad or uncaring bone in their bodies.

Of their seven children, my father was the firstborn. He came into the world on April 11, 1927. By April 12, 1927, he was trying to figure out a way to get something for nothing.

For as long as I can remember, I have been disgusted by those who use poverty or a dysfunctional home life as an excuse for their failings as a human being. I just hate it.

While various lowlifes regularly offer up those excuses for committing often heinous crimes, at least they do so from a foundation of real childhood dysfunction. A condition or reality that never existed for my dad.

What excuse can you offer up for horrendous behavior when you come from a family that was the Boston version of *Ozzie and Harriet*? None, other than that you have some severe character flaws that can't be fixed.

Off and on over the years, I have heard people say that some particular dirtbag was "just born bad." *Just born bad.* While it may be an oversimplification or impossible for most people to believe, at least for my dad, it seemed to be a title and explanation that fit.

The earth is full of real-life monsters. Monsters who had mommies and daddies, played with their toys as toddlers, wore cute little outfits, and then grew up to perpetrate some of the most heinous crimes known to humanity. While my dad was far removed from that type of Monster, he was still, at least in my opinion, a monster with a small *m*. He literally hurt, damaged, and bankrupted countless people along the way, as he did all in his power to satisfy his every vulgar need.

My uncle Peter once told me that his brother John—my dad—was the only person he had ever known in his entire life who did not have a conscience. Not one molecule of a conscience.

My father could stiff a little old lady out of her desperately needed rent money, defraud a small businessman of thousands of dollars, cheat on his wife, or steal from one of his siblings—or children—and not lose one second of sleep. Not one second. By any honest assessment, that is someone who is "born bad." Unfortunately for me, he was also born to be my father.

So, the more that various relatives test-drove lame excuses for my parents' unpardonable treatment of us, the more disappointed and angry I became. I *knew* better. I knew the absolute child-destroying facts.

My parents just didn't care. *Our* parents, the two people who brought us into the world, simply did not care.

When I say "did not care," I mean that in the strictest sense of the words. My parents did not care if we went days without food. My parents did not care if our clothes were filthy. My parents did not care if we smelled bad. My parents did not care if other children made constant fun of us. My parents did not care if we were jerked once again from our home, our school, and our friends. My parents did not care that our teeth were rotting out of our heads or causing us excruciating pain. My parents did not care . . . about us.

We were, at best, an annoyance. And at worst, we were . . . the *enemy.*

All of these relatives and friends who tried to explain away this illicit conduct collectively arrived at the same conclusion: "It's the booze. They would never treat you this way if they were sober."

What a load of crap. While those inventing the excuse may have had good intentions, they had not a clue. I knew what the truth was. And it is *that* truth that caused me so much pain.

That truth—THE truth—was that my parents were not drunk all the time. In fact, they were sober most of the time. Sober *most* of the time.

My dad was an interesting alcoholic. Unlike most drunks who dove into the bottle when times were bad, that is when my dad would buckle down, rip off half a dozen people, and *then* dive into said bottle.

My dad only drank when things were going great. At least *his* twisted definition of great. But when he did drink, he was a binge drinker. He would drink himself into an alcohol-induced haze that would last anywhere from two to six weeks. During this time, he would spend whatever money he had stolen from those gullible enough to trust him on women, trips, booze, and himself. Always and only on himself. Never on his wife or children.

When he did this, my brother, sister, and I would wait for the final curtain to come down: being evicted from yet another home; a forced trip into the unknown one more time.

During these episodes, my mom—not unexpectedly to some— also drank. But again, most times she also was sober.

Because of the life she had lived with *her* mother, my mom was not equipped to handle real life. Not by a long shot. She would much rather be Shirley Temple in *The Bachelor and the Bobby-Soxer*, or June Allyson in any movie with Van Johnson. She wanted to be the popular sorority girl who lands the big man on campus and then lives happily ever after.

My mom was an amazing artist and had an incredible skill for interior decorating. Unfortunately, her own damaged DNA and a cockroach of a husband got in the way of her talents and her fantasies for life. That and the three little rug rats who always seemed to want food, a hug, or any display of affection and love.

Tragically for her and for us, my mom's only solution to her cheating husband and the burst bubble that was her dream was to drink. And drink heavily.

Weirdly her drink of choice, just like my dad's, was vodka. She increased her consumption as the years went on so her fantasy could recede into nothing more than a booze-clouded fog.

With all of that, they were still more sober than drunk. *More sober than drunk.* And when they were sober, they realized *exactly* what kind of squalor their children were living in and how much emotional pain and damage they were causing. But guess what? Even sober, *they didn't care.*

My mother would actually—and I say this literally—treat stray cats with more love and compassion than she did any of her three children. Coming in a poor second to an alley cat. That is a tough truth to accept.

21

A Minority Greeting and a Beating

One of the real, honest-to-goodness positives that I got out of poverty was my exposure to minority America. For me, Hispanic and black America has always been and will always be a *great* America. And, with a few exceptions, it's an America about as far removed from the gangbanging stereotypes of Hollywood or the dishonest portrayal by the liberal mainstream media as it can get.

As we moved from town to town, I was often one of the few white kids in my class. I honestly never really noticed or cared what color my classmates were. I was just thrilled that, because they were just like me from a poverty sense, they didn't make fun of me. We shared the bond of abject poverty, and the power of that connection cannot be underestimated.

That is not to say that others did not notice the differences in skin color or seek out trouble and retribution, because surely some did. I just tried my best not to be on the receiving end of trouble or painful retribution.

My first real challenging, nerve-testing, intriguing, and rewarding experiences as one of the few white boys in class came in the tenth grade. It was one of those "exceptions." I was going to Dorchester High School at the time, and because the school was so crowded, they shuffled a bunch of us tenth graders off to an annex building down the street.

As it turned out, they mostly shuffled a bunch of hard-ass brothers to the annex and a few extras from *The Pillsbury Dough Boy—The Movie*. Those extras were me and a few other white guys.

The phrase that most sticks in my mind from that half year—we moved once again before I could finish my sentence—was "You know what time it is, Casper? It's time for you to give me a quarter, mother------!"

But . . . an ironic thing happened on the way to the ass-kicking. The brothers soon realized that I was *the* poorest white boy they had ever seen. And then something really strange happened. They basically adopted me as their pet.

Seriously. The tenth-grade annex for Dorchester High School became like a petting zoo with me as the white baby goat. These street-wise, very tough black guys—I swear a couple of them were in their early thirties—actually felt sorry for me. From that moment on, I was "protected." No one would extort me, jump me, or threaten me anymore. I was the poor, smelly white kid, and I guess the brothers felt that was punishment enough.

That same reasoning did not apply to the few other white boys in the annex. They got their butts kicked on such a regular basis, the brothers could set the watches they stole from their teachers on it.

One time in English class, five brothers walked in and closed the door. The only ones in the classroom were me and a semihard-ass white kid name Curt. It seemed Curt had dissed the brothers on occasion, and they didn't think that was such a good thing. They came into the classroom to demonstrate their displeasure at such an obvious and undignified affront.

Now you might be rightfully asking, "How could this go on right *inside* a classroom, *inside* a school, while school was *in session*. That's just not possible." Hah! Check your ignorance at the door along with your sense of right and wrong.

On this particular day, our teacher had once again called in sick. The substitute teacher had not shown up, and another teacher had poked her head into the classroom to address the five students who had bothered to show up. Once she announced that this was going to be a "free study period," the three other students split, leaving Curt and me to the classroom.

So here we were. Curt, myself, and five fairly big, pissed-off brothers. The ringleader of the brothers walked over to me and said, "This don't concern you, Casper, so mind your own business."

With that, two of the other brothers grabbed my arms and held me down at my desk to make sure I minded my own business. Once they dealt with me, the ringleader and the other two proceeded to kick the ever-loving snot out of Curt.

They punched him, bounced him, slammed him, threw chairs at him, and broke a three-foot-long wooden blackboard cleaner over his head. The beating was over in about sixty seconds. The brothers left Curt covered in his own blood, lying on the floor behind the teacher's desk, as they calmly walked back out to the busy hallway of Dorchester High School in search of their next victim.

Curt never came back to school after that experience, and I was *paroled* to yet another high school a few weeks later.

22

Rolling Pennies in the Dark

In many ways, abject poverty can be boiled down to a constant and even debilitating fear of the unknown. Such as the absolute terror produced from an unexpected knock at your door.

Famed British actor Michael Caine wrote about this fear in his exceptionally well-written and moving autobiography, *What's It All About?* The book details, among other things, his impoverished childhood in the east end of London. Caine not only talks about the fear that an unexpected knock causes, but credits his practiced answers to the bill collectors as the foundation for his impressive acting skills. At the age of five, he was protecting his mom.

Well, moms are moms. Be they in London, England, or in Dorchester, Massachusetts. Even if they are emotional cripples like my mom was, you still love them and do not want to see them in pain. No matter the pain inflicted upon me, I was still that lone baby bird with two broken wings trying to help the other birds. Even the ones who had damaged themselves and others.

While I never went into the acting profession, many of us who grew up in poverty know much more about acting, psychology, and human nature than most of the professionals in those fields. The education was free and came with the territory.

A year or so and a couple of moves after the beating of Curt, we hit what I considered to be the lowest of the lows. Rock bottom.

I was fifteen when one of those horrible and unexpected knocks at the door came our way.

My father was missing again. The electricity and phone had once again been shut off for nonpayment, and the landlord was pounding his fists on our back door, screaming at the top of his lungs. He wanted the months of rent owed him and demanded that we get out "immediately, before I throw you and your worthless possessions out on the sidewalk."

As he had already—*illegally*—shut off our water, which meant we had no running water to drink, wash dishes with, or flush the toilets with, I had no doubt that our eviction was just days away. In the midst of all of that nightmare, my mom and I found ourselves sitting at our kitchen table doing two sad and desperate things.

In the darkness of a kitchen illuminated only by two candles on the table, my mom and I sat and rolled pennies. We had a large jar between us on the table that contained several hundred pennies, and we were packing them into fifty-cent rolls and stacking the rolled pennies off to the side of the table.

We were rolling the pennies for two reasons. My sister was sick and needed some medicine and food. Ironically, the little food we did have had gone bad when our electricity was shut off.

People tend to be more focused and energized when they are involved in a mission to help others. As were my mom and I that night. Our mission was to make sure my little sister had her medicine and at least a little food, so she would not suffer more than she already had.

The other desperate act we were involved in that night was entering contests. Under the light of our candles, my mom and I entered over twenty contests. Unlike other—"normal"—people, who enter contests to win fabulous trips to Europe or luxury cars, we were entering these meager contests just to survive. Just to win *anything*.

My mom read and saved most of the women's magazines of the

day, everything from *Good Housekeeping* to *Redbook* to *McCall's*. And in each magazine there were usually a few contests for readers to enter. Nothing major. Just contests for furniture, magazine subscriptions, or other things we did not have and might be able to sell for money.

So in our hour of complete and utter desperation, and with my mom openly crying at that kitchen table because of how scared she was of the days to come, we entered as many contests as we could. To enter them meant simply clipping a small coupon from one of the magazines, filling it out with my mom's name and our address of the moment, then sticking said coupon in an envelope with a stamp. When all of them were ready, I dropped them into the local mailbox on my way to pick up my sister's medicine and some food.

When you are really poor—the kind of poor that was our everyday existence—you have nothing. Nothing but maybe a faint glimmer of hope. A hope that things will somehow get better. A hope that your mom and dad will finally stop drinking and learn to love, appreciate, or just feed you. At the very least . . . notice you.

You have a hope that the world and your fellow human beings won't be as cruel as they seem and that your life will eventually get better because it just can't get worse. When you are truly poor, you are guaranteed one thing: *nothing*. But contained in that nothing are minuscule hopes, dreams, and fantasies that will most likely never be realized.

It is those almost-impossible-to-realize hopes, dreams, and fantasies that allow you to go on. That give you the will to fight at least one more day.

If it were the movies or a good beach book, my mom and I would win multiple contests, and the prizes would turn our lives completely around. In reality, of course, we won nothing. Not a T-shirt, not a mug, not a free magazine subscription.

While we won nothing, we did gain something much more

precious than prizes: a faint glimmer of hope and fantasy. For days and weeks afterward, we were able to think, *What if? What if we win a living room set? What if we win an encyclopedia set? What if we actually win fifty thousand dollars?* It would have been all the money in the world to us.

When you live beneath the poverty line day after day, you need to give your mind some modicum of escape in order to survive. Mental escape means everything. Especially for a child.

It was for that very reason that I would get so angry when I'd hear some incredibly wealthy person or member of Congress berate the poor for having a color TV. Are you *kidding* me?

This condescending accusation from the ignorant usually went something like this: "Look at those people"—usually a euphemism for minorities—"they claim they can't afford to put food on the table and yet they've managed to buy themselves a *color* TV. They don't seem so poor to me."

Other than terminal stupidity, what gives them the right to speak like that? Why is it that those who know nothing about poverty are always so willing to speak against the poor and offer up worthless and, in fact, destructive solutions?

For "those people," their color TVs serve as a very limited escape, allowing many of them to make it through the day. So many times, the only smile or laugh they will have all day will come via an electronic window to a better and safer world than their own.

Unlike the rich person or member of Congress who criticizes them, they can't go see a play, go to the country club, drive to the mountains, fly to Europe, go on a taxpayer-funded junket, or do the hundreds of other things that people with "means" can do. More often than not, they literally can't even walk out of their apartments at night without fear of being shot.

Imagine that for a second. Please. Imagine that you are a parent and are petrified to have your child step just outside your front door because they may be killed. *Killed.* It may not happen in the suburbs or in the affluent congressional districts of America, but it's a reality and fear for thousands and thousands of Americans. Good Americans who typically work harder than most and still go way out of their way to practice that Golden Rule.

Yet knowing this awful reality, many in a position of power or means purposefully attack the poor for seeking out a relatively inexpensive and quite sad means of escape.

Pathetic is too kind a word for their misplaced ignorance and condemnation.

23

The Deception That Gave Me a Chance

Ironically, the last and most effective push that steered me away from a possible life of crime and more poverty was the chance to go to school with some relatively rich white kids.

Soon after the night of rolling pennies and filling out contest forms, our very angry landlord succeeded—they always do—in having us evicted. We had been there for about six months, so this was basically right on our eviction schedule.

I was attending Roslindale High School in Boston at the time, a school I mostly enjoyed and where I started running track as a way to escape a few more hours of home life.

Just prior to our eviction, my dad mysteriously reappeared just as quickly as he had disappeared. When he did, he greeted us with the news that he was moving us to a very affluent suburb of Boston, called Westwood. Westwood had a ton of money and one of the best public high schools in the state—both for academics and for sports.

Of course, the only way my dad could pull this off was by passing a bad check or by scraping together the first month's rent and then passing his worthless checks. It would not take the owner long to figure out he had been scammed and start the eviction process. Until then, I intended to soak in the many benefits of this upscale town, the magnificent home, and the Norman Rockwell–like neighborhood.

Two great things immediately resulted from living in West-wood. The first was that it was about sixteen miles from Boston and the bad elements that could still prove a temptation for me. Second, even though I automatically qualified as the poorest kid in this very rich high school, I felt instantly at home. For the first time in my school life—having just turned sixteen—I felt totally at home in an upscale school. It was very strange and very comforting.

Part of the reason was the teachers. They were exceptional. This was a time prior to political correctness when most teachers valued the well-being of a student over the unethical demands of corrupt teachers' unions.

Because it was an affluent high school, Westwood tended to get very good teachers who did not need many things spelled out for them: chiefly, that I came before them with a number of serious and chronic issues.

Rather than ignore me, to a person they embraced me and tried to understand my problems and pain. Aside from feeling bad about my poverty, they detected some signs of intelligence and sought to cultivate my potential.

It was about this time that I also discovered that I was a fairly good athlete. So suddenly, coaches liked me as well. I quickly came to the conclusion that if I were ever going to get out of the canyon of despondency my parents had dug for me, Westwood High School had all the ingredients to provide the perfect lift.

Of course, my family being my family, we moved three more times before I had a chance to graduate from the school. That and, oh yeah, my father deserted us once again and then stole my grant money for college.

In order to stay at the school I now loved and saw as my salvation, I had to go to great pains not only to get there but also to hide the fact that I no longer lived in the town. If the school officials found out that my family no longer lived in Westwood, I would have been kicked out immediately.

In one case, we moved to a neighboring town called Dedham. I quickly figured out which Westwood school bus went to the border of Dedham nearest us. I took that bus every day after school and walked the approximately three miles to my home in Dedham. Come morning, I would do the reverse.

Once at Westwood, my raw talent for running track blossomed, and I became one of the "stars" on the track team, earning a couple of varsity letters in the process. I was finally able to put my skill at running from thugs and the police to good use. I never thought I'd even *see* a varsity letter, let alone earn one.

But besides any athletic acclaim I may have found at Westwood High School, I received two gifts infinitely more valuable: acceptance and peace of mind.

Certainly, both the very wealthy and the middle-class students I came in contact with on a daily basis at school could see that I was poor and going through tough times at home. A few even knew my secret about walking several miles a day from another town just to stay in school—which was straight out of a dream for me.

I have no doubts that they made comments about me to each other—and rendered a few harsh judgments based on my less than clean and polished appearance. But not once did anyone say anything negative or remotely condescending to me. It was a wonderful experience with some great teachers and classmates, and it gave me a welcome and much-needed opportunity to take a deep breath, relax, and actually have some fun. More than that, the experience put me on a foundation of normalcy.

That said, I had to struggle to climb up on that foundation each and every day, and I had to fight to stay there once on it. Between having to walk those endless miles each week, keeping the secret of why I needed to make those walks, and enduring the ever-growing dysfunction at home, I was always on the verge of losing that mental battle.

I am a person of tremendous faith. So after each day's forced walk to the edge of Westwood and back—often sandwiched around ten-mile runs for the track team—and after each ceramic cup of vodka hurled at my head once home, I would walk upstairs to our room and say a little prayer to my latest Baby Jesus for the strength needed to reach and then survive the next day.

In ways that I will never fully understand, He did give me that strength, and at sixteen and seventeen years of age, Westwood High School, its teachers, and many of its students provided me with the critical proof that my home life was abnormal to the extreme and that better things awaited me—if only I would seek them out. Westwood was a timely and inspirational launching pad.

24

Writing a Novel at Seventeen

Today, many Americans don't read. As a people and a nation, we are *way* too cool or busy for that. Ironically, those who need the escape and magic of the written word the most are the poor—and many rarely crack a book. Instead, exploitative television, twisted and violent music and video games, and life on the street corners are atrophying the minds of America's young poor.

Because books and reading had frequently offered me that much-needed oasis in the desert, I decided that maybe, just maybe, I could write one of these things myself. I decided this at the ripe old age of seventeen.

The book was called *Caper* and was about four college students—two couples—robbing the Museum of Fine Arts in Boston. I actually wanted to become an astronaut, but if that career didn't pan out, I had the solid backup plan of becoming a master criminal and jewel thief. Beating the system on a much larger stage with much more at stake.

As stated, one of my fictional favorites at the time was a character on the television show *It Takes a Thief.* Alexander Mundy was played by the very sophisticated Robert Wagner. Thanks to that show and a few memorable and inspirational films, I thought master criminal and jewel thief would be a great career move should the astronaut gig go south.

Because of that thinking and also because my favorite author was Donald E. Westlake—the best writer of comedic crime novels ever—I decided my first novel would be about robbing a famous museum in Boston.

The next step, of course, was to do the research needed for the book. While I may have been serious about the research, the real motivation to do it was to fool my mind and provide a few hours of escape from the ever-escalating insanity at home.

So I found myself taking public transportation to the museum to "case the joint." After several trips to the museum and looking into every dark corner and behind every doorway I could find— even hiding after hours in the museum—I sat down to write my first novel.

The main reason that I hid in the museum involves a rare very pleasant memory of time with my mom. I remember on a couple of occasions as a young boy watching the movie *How to Steal a Million* with her. The movie starred Audrey Hepburn—the gold standard for elegance and class, from whom years later I got a kiss on the cheek—and Peter O'Toole. My mom, who went to finishing school and was a very sophisticated woman when lucid, was a huge fan of Hepburn and felt I should be introduced to such grace. I was glad she did.

Naturally, that movie was about robbing an art museum in Paris. Naturally, Hepburn and O'Toole had to hide in the museum after hours. Naturally, I had to replicate that act by hiding after hours in the Museum of Fine Arts in Boston. So, naturally, I did. Undetected and quite proud of my skullduggery.

I did so as research for my little novel, as an homage to one of my all-time favorite movies and, strangely, as a way to build on that wonderful memory with my mom.

• • •

Not only did I sit down to write this little novel, but more important, I finished it. Six months or so after I started, and now at the age of eighteen, I had a completed forty-thousand-word manuscript sitting on my table. It may have qualified as the worst novel ever written, but written and finished it was.

Much more than proving that I had the discipline needed to finish, the very process underscored and proved the power and healing effects of the written word.

A lesson that must be learned by the poor of this world.

25

The Square Peg in the Round Hole of College

With graduation from Westwood High School looming, I knew I needed to get into a fairly good college to enhance my chances of escape from what was nothing more than an imitation of an existence. More than that, I knew it was critical that I *physically* leave my home for the peace of mind that would greet me upon moving into a college dorm. While that was a logical plan, things did not work out that way. Not even close.

I was fortunate enough to be accepted to some good colleges both near and relatively far from my home. Because my now fourteen-year-old sister was still at home (Jay started staying with friends regularly by the time he was sixteen, and by eighteen had moved out permanently) and in the center of the storm, I knew I could not go far, lest I be needed quickly for a rescue.

With that guaranteed eventuality in mind, I chose a college about forty miles from Boston. So at the age of seventeen going on one thousand, I moved into my first, and last, college dorm.

As expected, the college assigned me a roommate who was a year or so older and seemed to come from a great deal of money. From the very first day we were introduced, he looked down on me and regularly made derogatory comments—almost always in front of other students—about my clothes, my upbringing, and the smell that sometimes still emanated from my body. The unfair and hurtful judgments never seemed to stop.

So . . . after the mental respite and partial rejuvenation that was Westwood High School, I was catapulted right back into the snob factory. Great.

Leaving aside the verbal bullying for the moment, as a newly minted college freshman, living on my own for the first time, I still had much to learn. One of those lessons was not to overload myself by taking on more than I could handle. It was a lesson I was about to learn the hard way.

Because of the life I had led up until that point, I knew I was far behind the eight-ball and that many other students were far ahead of me on the academic and life scale. So my thinking was that I would have to double up just to catch them. Part of that thinking came from necessity and part from arrogance.

My dad never gave me anything out of kindness or in the role of the parent. But one of the things I apparently did inherit from him was a fairly high IQ. While life had stripped me bare of any luxuries, God seemed to have given me a somewhat decent and quick mind to cope with the incoming fire that always rained down upon me.

For the obvious reasons of abject poverty and the fact that I was a dreamer who always looked out the window, I was almost never anything approaching an A student. Even at that, if angered or motivated, I could turn it on at will and surprise people on purpose.

Once, as a younger child in Catholic school, Sister Mary-Crazy had browbeat me to the point where I simply went on strike. I finally just sat at my desk day after day and refused to do one bit of school work. No matter how much they yelled, I sat with my hands folded on my desk and didn't do a thing. Nothing.

This went on for weeks. Finally, the mother superior decided to move me up to the next grade for the rest of the school year to see what would happen. The second she did, I banged out straight A's as a way of proving they had no understanding of me and even less control.

Years later, I had to take my first actual IQ test. The result seemed to shock the teachers and administration in a good way. So much so, that without asking me or getting my permission, they announced my score over the loudspeaker to the entire school. While most might be proud with the result and public announcement, I was horrified with the breach of my privacy. Privacy was one of my most protective shields; the less people knew about me, the less they could hurt me.

Five seconds after the announcement, all of the students in my class turned to look at me and started to whisper to each other. I felt my face turning bright red as my ears started to burn. I instantly grabbed my book bag and ran out of the school and did not return until a week later, after my brother had convinced me the administrators would apologize to me upon my arrival. Of course, when I went back, that never happened. Creeps.

Some native intelligence and confidence—occasionally bolstered by a healthy portion of arrogance—can be good things, as long as the limits are understood and respected. I went past one of those limits my first days in college when I foolishly decided to take twenty-one credits my first semester, become a physics major, enroll in Air Force ROTC, and play ice hockey for a junior-A team up the street. All of that with the daily crap still happening at home. Can you say "overload"?

On top of that, after about a month of living in the dorm room with my constantly needling and snotty roommate, a minor confrontation ensued. While I could excuse the confrontation as a result of the stress and exhaustion, that would not be entirely accurate or fair.

The simple truth was that my roommate was a privileged and pampered jerk, and I had reached the point of no return with his constant and demeaning insults. Unfortunately for him, he had three things working against him when he dropped that last straw on the camel's deeply swayed back.

First, while he was a verbal bully empowered by elitism and status, he was a physical wimp in all other respects. Second, while now off the sometimes very mean streets of Dorchester, I still had the survival instincts of a Dorchester rat and could and would still strike out when cornered or threatened. Last, during the summer between my junior and senior year of high school, I had gone from a fairly scrawny five-ten and 150 pounds to about six-two and about 175 pounds. Now as a freshman in college who was hitting the weights on a regular basis, I was topping out at something over 180 pounds.

What sparked this predestined confrontation was my still evolving sense of hygiene combined with his pretentious antics. While I was getting better at taking care of myself, I knew I still had a way to go to match the standards of "civilized" society.

I was thrilled to have regular hot water for the first time in my life and was showering every morning and brushing my teeth afterward. What I was *not* doing was washing my clothes. That required quarters for the machines, and I simply did not have the money.

Before I even started college, my dad stole the grant money I had received to pay my first year's tuition. Consequently, the summer after graduating high school I worked at a local department store as well as at a local restaurant as a dishwasher and busboy just to resave the money needed to pay for my first semester.

Beyond that, I had not one dime extra for anything. Not snacks, not sodas, not a movie. The only food I got was the two meals a day I was entitled to thanks to my college meal ticket. While my dorm mates would regularly buy themselves subs, sodas, and even beer, I did without. It was not like I was going to get a check or even a dollar sent to me from home.

Because I had no extra quarters for washing machines, my clothes, and especially my socks, soon became gamey. While not the brightest bulb in the marquee of life, I was also not a complete idiot. I knew my clothes were dirty, and I knew the smell offended my roommate, as he would tell me several times a day.

Finally, fueled by pride and shame, I started sneaking down to the shower room to try to wash my socks and underwear by hand in the sink with my bar of soap. Unfortunately, that was not enough for my roommate.

One night after coming back to our room from studying late on campus, I changed my clothes and climbed up into my top bunk to go to sleep. I guess the smell of my socks and my sneakers proved too much for my roommate.

He soon jumped out of the bottom bunk, grabbed his bottle of aftershave off his desk, opened it, and poured the entire contents all over me and my blanket. Bad move.

I guess he thought I would just take it. He was wrong. I sprang from my bunk, hit the floor, wrapped my left hand around his throat, shoved him into his metal locker next to his desk, and punched him—just once—in the solar plexus.

He collapsed onto the floor and started to curl up like a piece of bacon on a frying pan as he struggled to get back the breath that had been knocked completely out of him.

Nobody had to tell me I was wrong for what I did. I knew I was wrong. Unfortunately for my roommate, he was the catalyst that caused me to snap.

I soon picked him up off the floor, apologized, and deposited him back into his bunk. I explained to him in a very serious tone that I had had enough of his insulting comments and elitist attitude and that I was doing the best I could under very trying circumstances.

After that night, while never buddies, we did settle into an uneasy but workable truce.

26

A Bridge Too High

Because of my love of space and all things science, I had decided at the age of seventeen that I, in fact, did want to become an astronaut. Period. To reach that lofty goal, I knew I had to become a pilot—Air Force or Navy—and then log thousands of hours of flight time and experience before NASA would even consider my application.

When I was ten, I became enthralled with spaceflight and did something most normal kids would not—no surprise here. I started a scrapbook on the Soviet space program. Not ours, but the Soviet program. I think I did so because their program was shrouded by so much mystery at the time, and I had always wanted to solve mysteries. By the time I was a freshman at college, I had compiled several scrapbooks on their program and was more committed to my dream than ever.

Once accepted to the college forty miles from home, I immediately enrolled in the Air Force ROTC program. I wanted and needed to become an astronaut, and the Air Force was a means to that end. It could qualify me for NASA, and at the time, it still had its own manned program.

Very sadly for me, my career with the Air Force did not last long. My dream of becoming an astronaut quickly went up in smoke. The fault for this flameout was mine and mine alone.

At the time—and truth be told, today as well—I *really* had trouble taking orders or directions from those who clearly didn't have a clue concerning what they were talking about or from those who came by their rank or privilege based on birthright, connections, or both.

Even though I was in Air Force ROTC, I didn't like to wear the uniform on campus. Don't get me wrong, I was very proud to be in the organization, and was *very* proud of the uniform and everything it represented. It was just that some college students—including my obnoxious roommate—who were not in the program and who were still caught up in the antiwar movement would harass me and others who wore the uniform. We only had to wear the uniform on Tuesdays, but every time I wore it, I took grief from some antimilitary moron who had a grudge against the United States.

Since it was now fall, we also had to wear a topcoat over our uniform. The topcoat was very cool, so my compromise was to just not wear my Air Force cap.

After years of abuse and poverty as a child and young adult, I was in no mood to listen to some loser on campus call me a "warmonger."

So on this particular Tuesday, as I was walking in full uniform, minus the cap, from my dorm to the main campus, I was in a very good mood. I was looking forward to Friday, when we would go up to Pease Air Force Base in New Hampshire to fly in some C-130s. At this point in life, the only thing that kept me going was my love of flying and my desire to become a pilot and then an astronaut.

To get to the main campus from my dorm, I had to cross a bridge that spanned a river about a hundred feet below. Just about halfway across the bridge, a junior who was also in Air Force ROTC was crossing toward me from the other side. He walked up to me and said, "Where is your cap, mister?"

I explained to this guy—who at least in ROTC outranked me,

but was less than vermin in all other respects—that I would prefer not to wear my cap when I walked to class. He then proceeded to go Rambo on my ass, saying that I was disrespecting the uniform and that I was a bad "candidate officer." He then told me that as punishment, I would not be allowed to go to Pease Air Force Base on Friday and go flying.

As I had already lost out on a chance to attend the U.S. Air Force Academy because of my dysfunctional home life, I strongly believed this was the best and last ticket for me to escape poverty and help my family. So . . . another bad thing to say.

I asked him politely to reconsider. I explained that it was incredibly important that I go flying and that I would try to wear my cap from now on.

No joy. He screamed, "Not a chance, pal!" and said it was "too late." Then he said, "Someone like you has no business being in our program." As he started to walk past me on his way to the dorm, I decided to see if I could make him reconsider his decision. The method I chose—granted, not the smartest thing I've ever done—was to grab him from behind, drag him to the rail of the bridge, and dangle him a hundred feet over the rocks and rushing water below as I asked him one more time if he might change his mind.

Safe to assume, I didn't get to go flying that Friday. In fact, I was asked to leave the program immediately. The irony of the situation was that while I had the highest grades for classes related to ROTC, I was told I had also set the school record for demerits.

27

The Agency Offers an Out

Sometime after college, and after flailing about a bit more, I received the most interesting letter of my life to that point.

It was from the personnel representative of the Boston office of the Central Intelligence Agency. The letter read:

Dear Mr. MacKinnon:

It has come to my attention that your background may be of employment interest to the Central Intelligence Agency.

Before an appointment to this Agency is made, it is usually necessary to complete: a local interview, completion of formal applications, testing, background investigations, and headquarters interviews. In all, it generally requires 80–120 days after our local interview before we can make a formal employment commitment.

Please call this office to establish an interview date in Boston. Should any of these procedures preclude your interest or availability, please let me know. I hope this letter may be an initial step in exploring a rewarding and challenging career.

Sincerely yours,
Charles P——

Very strange, to say the least. Strange for several reasons. First, my mother, sister, and I had just moved . . . again.

We had not yet gone to the post office to leave a forwarding address and, for the usual reasons of rent money owed, had not left a forwarding address with our former landlord. Had he known, I'm sure he would have shown up at our new front door with all the other landlords we had stiffed over the years. All would be quite angry, all would be carrying pitchforks and torches, and all would be demanding to "see the Monster."

No. We never left forwarding addresses.

And yet, even though we had just moved to this new apartment two weeks earlier, the letter from the CIA had arrived at our *current* address.

The second strange reason was the obvious question most people would ask themselves: "Why me?"

Even though still wet behind the ears, I knew a few things about "Spook Central." Most of my information had been gleaned from Bond flicks; television shows such as *Get Smart, Mission: Impossible,* and *It Takes a Thief;* and various comic books. I may not have been an expert, but I considered myself close. How could I not with that highly exclusive research material at my fingertips?

So, again. "Why me?" Because of that meticulous research, I knew the CIA *always* recruited Ivy League types with wonderful tans, clefts in their chins, homes in the Hamptons, and the number III after their last names. You know . . . trust-fund babies.

Let's look at *my* qualifications for a second. I was dirt poor, had a GPA from a low-level state college you needed a microscope to view, and had been on the edge of criminal behavior for much of my young life. As for the Ivy League, they wouldn't let someone like me clean the toilets of Harvard, much less attend. Hardly CIA material.

After getting the letter, my first thought was that it was clearly a mistake. There must be another Douglas MacKinnon in Boston.

A rich, tanned, lockjawed version of me without the baggage. Must be. Somehow, I got his letter by mistake.

I put the letter aside and tried to ignore it. Hah! *You* try ignoring a letter from the CIA. It ain't easy. For all I knew, if I didn't call this guy within a couple of days, the poison they coated the letter with would be activated, and they wouldn't give me the antidote unless I signed my name in blood.

Since I did not want that to happen, I called Charles P. at the phone number listed on the upper-right-hand corner of his letter. I got a secretary and gave my name, and he was on the line five seconds later. "Mr. MacKinnon. It's very nice to hear from you."

Sounded Ivy League. Civilized, clipped words with a tinge of "I'm so much better than you" hanging in the air.

After a bit more of the required small talk, I made an appointment to go downtown to meet Mr. P.

The stationery they sent my letter on was telling. On the very top, all in black letters and capitalized, were the words CENTRAL INTELLIGENCE AGENCY. Centered just below that in smaller black caps were WASHINGTON, D.C. 20505.

The only address listed for the Boston office was in the upper-right-hand corner of the letter above the phone number. And that address was only a PO box. Since I couldn't show up at a PO box, they were forced to give me an *actual* address. They didn't seem to like it, but since *they* wanted to meet *me,* they spit it out and asked me to keep it confidential.

The following week, I took a city bus to the local T station and then took the T to the State Street station in downtown Boston. No surprise, I was going to the John F. Kennedy Federal Office Building, located next to city hall.

I was half hoping that, like Maxwell Smart, I would walk through a series of doors that slammed behind me until I got to the phone booth at the end, where I would dial a special number and drop through the floor, down a tube, and on my way to my secret appointment.

No such luck. I walked into the building and took the elevator up a few floors, then walked out into a nondescript office suite, with a nondescript receptionist. I gave my nondescript name and was told to take a seat.

No sooner had I started to flip through the latest *Sports Illustrated* when Mr. P. poked his head out of his office and called for me. I walked into his office and closed the door behind me. Again I was greeted with disappointment. No "cone of silence," no secret gadgets, and no Bat phone. I was starting to have serious doubts regarding my years of research.

Mr. P. was fairly tall, thin, well dressed, had thick salt-and-pepper hair, and looked like a Hollywood version of an Ivy League professor. At least I still had *that* part right. He directed me to one of the two chairs in front of his desk.

The conversation went something like this:

"Thank you for coming in," he said.

"You're welcome. I guess I only have one question before we start. And that is—"

Mr. P. cut me off. "Why you?"

I nodded and said nothing.

"Mr. MacKinnon. Doug. Do you mind if I'm totally frank with you?"

Nothing good ever follows a question like that, but I again nodded my head, while taking a second to make note of all the exits in case things got appreciably weirder.

When you grow up in less than idyllic circumstances with less than civilized people, just about the time you learn to walk, you train your mind to look for all potential avenues of escape as well as all potential weapons.

With that survival task in mind, I quickly cataloged that Mr. P. had a long steel letter opener, a sharp fountain pen, and several newly sharpened pencils on his desk. Clearly, in the country clubs he inhabited in his youth, he never had to worry about escape or makeshift weapons of self-defense.

He clapped his hands together and brought me back to my strange reality. "Good. Let me give you a thumbnail sketch of things and then answer why we reached out to you."

I actually found myself inching forward in my seat. Both out of curiosity and in case I had to spring out of my chair for any number of wild scenarios now bouncing around my tiny little mind.

"My job," he began, "is to find two types of employee for the Central Intelligence Agency. The first is the analyst type. You know, the ones who work at headquarters and analyze the millions of bits of information that come pouring in every day. By far, the analyst positions represent the largest percentage of our employees."

The more I inched forward in my chair, the more he leaned back in his very comfortable-looking black leather chair. Maybe I should have had a mint before coming into the office.

"The second position, the one that is always misportrayed in movies and books, is that of a field agent. Meaning, of course, someone who works overseas, generally undercover, and gathers information that is critical to the defense of the United States. It is that position, and our need to fill some openings, that brings you here today."

I decided on the spot that I really didn't want to know *why* they suddenly had openings to fill. Don't forget that by eighteen, I had already completed my first novel, and my imagination was still in fine working order. Sitting before Mr. P. in the Boston field office of the Central Intelligence Agency had automatically shifted my worst-case scenario into fifth gear. Details, I could do without.

"So, why me for *that* position?" I managed to croak out.

He folded his hands before him on his desk and smiled at me. "Again, Doug. Is it all right if I'm perfectly honest with you?"

"Yes, sir," I answered.

He nodded his head and continued. "Because, to put it as bluntly as possible"—and he used much more colorful and profane language than I am relating here—"you're a mess. Your family life is a joke, and near as I can tell, your future is preordained for failure."

Wow, I thought. Had I known *that* was a qualification for government work, I would have started screwing things up years earlier. Maybe I could have been in Congress by now.

He continued. "Without naming names, a former professor of yours brought your, ah, *situation* to our attention. Since then, we've kept an eye on you. And what we've seen indicates to us that you would operate well in the field."

What's that? I thought. *That on most days I look like Pig-Pen from Charlie Brown and could therefore be invisible to the enemy?* That's what I *thought*. What I said was "Why?"

"Why? Because you've dealt with just about every horrible situation life can throw at you at a young age, and you keep surviving. No matter what the situation or how quickly it changes, you adapt. You adapt, you learn, and you grow stronger. To say the least, you seem to think very quickly on your feet. All qualifications that would make for an excellent field agent."

Perfect. So all this time I thought Mom and Dad were destroying my life with neglect and poverty, when in reality they were establishing my qualifications for dangerous government work in faraway lands. I made a mental note to thank them when they sobered up.

After a few more minutes of dazed conversation, I left the office and made my way back home, with the promise that I would call him soon.

Weeks went past as I considered my options. On a blank piece of paper, I listed said options. On the right side, I listed the CIA. On the left side, I listed all my other options. Not surprisingly, that side of the page was blank. As white and devoid of contrast as nineteen polar bears frolicking in a snowbank during a blizzard. (All props here to Apollo 11 Command Module Pilot Mike Collins.)

Okay. Decision made. I wanted out of my horrible existence in the worst way possible, and the CIA was throwing me a lifeline. I decided to grab on with both hands and let it drag me away from my everyday anguish.

A few weeks after reconnecting, I found myself down in Rosslyn, Virginia, being subjected to a two-day physical at an office building the CIA had transformed into their very own mini-medical clinic. The thousands of people who poured out of the Metro station one block away were completely ignorant of the fact that their tax dollars were hard at work in a secret medical facility that was screening future secret agents or not-so-secret analysts. Shhhhh!

After two days of letting these doctors do things to me they wouldn't do to a lab rat, it was off to CIA headquarters in Langley, Virginia. There I was subjected to interviews, a polygraph, more interviews, and a detailed explanation of what would be expected of me as an employee of the Central Intelligence Agency.

As it turned out, the examiner I got for my polygraph was not an altogether normal guy. He felt it necessary to do a card trick for me. He put a blood pressure cuff on my arm, hooked up my fingertips, and put that cord around my chest.

"Now, Mr. MacKinnon," the rodent-looking man said in a numbing monotone, "I'm going to show you why it is a total waste of time trying to lie to us."

It sort of hurt my feelings that after looking me up and down, he automatically assumed I'd be lying to him. Bet he didn't think that way of the Ivy League types.

Rodent-man then gave me a deck of cards and asked me to pick one out, look at it, and put it back in the deck.

Once done, he then named off every card in the deck and asked if it were my card. I was instructed to say "No" every time. Thereby exposing my lie. Well sure enough, he got me. He looked at his little graph paper and said: "Your card is the two of spades."

I just smiled up at him. "Hey, no kidding? Listen, let me ask you a question. Does Doug Henning know you're doing his act?"

Not even a hint of a smile in return. In fact, he looked at me like I was something that needed to be scraped off the bottom of his shoe.

This guy may have had great confidence in his machine and his ability to interpret the squiggles it produced, but soon after the exam, I found out that it was subjectively accurate. It depended, in large measure, upon the person taking the test, and his or her ability to tell the truth, lie, or be influenced by nerves.

After taking the test, I was left alone in the room for about a half hour to contemplate life. As I continued my rather pedestrian thought process, the lie detector technician walked in with his supervisor to announce in a very loud voice that I had failed the test. His revenge for my joke.

As my career of last resort burst into flames before my eyes, I managed to squeak out, "How? Why? I didn't lie about anything. Maybe you need a new machine, or you need to go back to lie-detector school or something."

He now leered at me with the look of someone who just stopped a crime in progress.

"Drugs," he said as he energetically nodded his thin head up and down. "You lied to us about your past drug use."

"What?" I screamed. "Look, you're the one on drugs if you think I ever used drugs."

I was more than ready to go down for something I had done wrong, but I had never done drugs in my life. Not once. Never.

After continued, earnest protesting on my part, they retested me and determined that because, as a teen, I had hung around hard-core drug users—and even held the spoon for them as they melted their heroin over an open flame—my background had caused me to fail the drug use part of the exam.

•   •   •

During this first visit to Langley, I was pretty sure the Agency also put me through an unannounced "ethics" test. Meaning they wanted to test my integrity and character in the most basic way possible.

During my processing, I was sent to meet with a stunning woman by the name of Donna. And when I say "stunning," I mean Miss Universe stunning. She was tall, had an incredible figure, and was wearing a very revealing dress better suited for a nightclub. She didn't seem like the "government type," unless the CIA was recruiting ex-showgirls from Las Vegas. No matter; as a red-blooded American male, I was very happy to see her.

Miss Las Vegas had me sit in a chair in front of her desk and asked me to give her my receipts for all of my expenses. She then did something that about had me fall out of that chair. She opened a drawer in her desk that was full—and I'm talking to the tippy-top—of cash. There had to be thousands of dollars in bills in that drawer, and I was the only one in the room who found that unusual. I guess checks and the CIA just didn't mix.

For sure, that was a Kodak moment for the memory bank. A stunning Vegas strip girl CIA employee smiling at me with her right hand holding open a drawer full of cash. Even with these visual delights before me, the street kid in me immediately pressed the "suspicious" button. As in, if it looks too good to be true, it most likely is not true.

After handing her the few crumpled receipts I had for the few dollars I was owed, she reached over and touched my hand. She then looked over at me with her perfect face and arctic blue eyes and said, "Are you *sure* this is all we owe you? Are you *really* sure. Even if you lost your receipts and just want to tell me how much else we owe you, I'll just give you that in cash right now. It's that easy, sugar. *Any* amount."

Ah-hah, I thought. *The weasel test come to fruition. I'm barely in the world of all things CIA and already they want to find out if I'm creep*

enough to cheat on my expenses. Well not me, sister. No way. I'm not
about to lose a great government career for a couple hundred bucks.

Of course, years later, I found out that it wasn't a test at all and
that the extra "expense" money would have been mine for the
taking. I still wouldn't have taken it, but knowing it was not a test
would have made me less paranoid as the rest of the process went
forward. After completing the testing and processing at Langley,
it was time to head home to Boston and pack the few possessions
I owned into a trash-can liner so I could move to Washington in
anticipation of my new career. As I was quite anxious to leave the
bad memories of my childhood behind me, I spent only a week
in Boston. Just enough time to say my good-byes and head right
back to D.C.

As it turned out, a career with the CIA was not in that deck of
cards for me. That said, I deeply believe that the Central Intelligence Agency serves as the most valuable and necessary branch of
our government. Period. In a world gone mad, our very existence
depends on the honorable men and women who work for this
much maligned, often scapegoated, and always misunderstood
agency.

Day in and day out, they do the toughest of jobs in some of the
most trying conditions and in some of the most inhospitable places
imaginable. They do this not for money, "glamour," or fame. And
certainly not for the credit. Rather, they do it for the most noble
of reasons: they are patriots.

How easy it is for some in Congress, the media, and the Hollywood elite to mock what the CIA represents and belittle the risks
taken by those who chose a different path. A path of honor, service, sacrifice, and sadly, sometimes a path of death. And usually
anonymous death at that.

I will always be deeply humbled and honored, that for a moment in time, the Central Intelligence Agency thought I could be among their number. May God bless and protect them all.

Soon thereafter, I had to deal with something I had feared my whole life: the loss of our mom.

At fifty-eight, she lost her battle with the bottle and had finally succumbed to cirrhosis. My sister, Janice, bravely took care of her up until the last minute.

The tragedy within the tragedy of my mom's passing was that *she* had lost her mom to cirrhosis when *her* mom was fifty-eight. Too bizarre and troubling for words.

While it was officially cirrhosis, I will always believe that she lost her battle to a broken heart. As she told it, she met my father when they both were three years old and had been in love with him ever since. Her twisted and irrational devotion and love to her despicable husband was unbreakable; so with each affair he had, each lost job, each arrest, and each eviction, another piece of her was permanently destroyed. It was only a matter of time.

She had all the potential in the world and deserved so much more out of life. Unfortunately, because of that all-consuming but misdirected love, she allowed my father to drag her down to his level.

With all of that, she was and still is my mom and I love her. I was born on *her* birthday. I inherited some of *her* incredible talent to draw and paint. I was—as she always called me as a child when she was sober and lucid—her "Little Lamb."

With her passing, my long-held fear was realized. I would never find out from her what I had done so wrong as a small child to be so undeserving of a mother. To be so undeserving of her love. To be so undeserving of . . . life.

The answers . . . her answers . . . went with her.

28

A Campaign Door Leads
to the White House

In the mid-1980s, a gentleman by the name of Andrew H. Card Jr. was working in the White House as a special assistant to President Ronald Reagan. Andy's turf was governors.

It was his job to keep the nation's governors informed as to what the president was up to and to take any issues or complaints they might have back to the White House. Andy was well qualified for the job for a number of reasons, not the least of which was that he had run for governor of Massachusetts as a state delegate.

Since Andy was from Massachusetts and a Republican, it is probably no surprise that we knew each other. Back then, you could have fit most of the Massachusetts Republican Party in a rowboat and still have had plenty of room for the cast of *Gilligan's Island*.

At one point around that time when I had come to the Reagan White House for a meeting on the space program—I had parlayed my childhood passion for human spaceflight into an understanding of the pros and cons of our space program, which enabled me to author a number of columns and articles on the subject, hence my invitation to the White House—I stopped by Andy's office to catch up. Andy's idea of catching up was to give me a quiz about Vice President George H. W. Bush. In retrospect, I have come to realize that Andy was giving me a loyalty test. I just wasn't bright enough to figure it out at the time.

After getting talk of the Red Sox and Bruins out of the way, Andy came right to the point.

"Doug." He smiled. "What do you think of Vice President Bush? And by that, I mean what do you *really* think of him? Do you think he has what it takes to be president of the United States, and would you support him?"

Little did I know that Andy was already like a son to Vice President Bush. Even though he worked for Ronald Reagan, Andy's first loyalty was to the vice president and his coming campaign.

The fact was, I did think well of Vice President Bush. Even though his world of wealth, titles, and connections was light-years removed from my life, I knew he had fought bravely for his country, tried to establish his own identity, and had lost a four-year-old daughter to disease. Rich or poor, God and life have a way of deciding how much pain and suffering to send your way, and both had sent some to Vice President Bush and his family.

I told Andy I thought the vice president was a good man and that I would be interested in helping out on his campaign if the right opportunity arose. Andy nodded his head, smiled, and told me he would be in touch. Of course, if I had given the wrong answer about Vice President Bush, then friends or not, Andy would have stuck me on the next yak to Siberia.

A few months after my conversation with Andy, I got a call from someone connected with Vice President Bush, asking if I would like to be a writer on the campaign. *Would I like to be a writer?*

I would have been thrilled if they said they had some wastebaskets that needed to be emptied for six dollars an hour. The presidential campaign of the sitting vice president is a very special place to be; knowing that, I jumped at the offer and in the process put my professional journey on a very interesting path.

So in late 1986, I moved back to Washington and joined not the Bush campaign but the Bush political action committee. It was called the Fund for America's Future. It could have been called the "Fund to Fund a Fund to Fund People Who Like Elmer Fudd" for all I cared. I was working on a Republican presidential campaign where traditional beliefs were supposed to be valued, honored, and followed. And to my surprise and satisfaction, a few of them actually were.

Several months into my new job, a low-level writing job opened up at the Reagan White House. Several senior Bush campaign people thought I should fill it, both because it would be great experience and because I could quite possibly spy on the Reaganites within the White House to hear if—as the rumors reported—they were saying anything negative about Vice President Bush.

The higher-ups at the Bush campaign didn't know I was already a huge admirer of President Ronald Reagan; and once I was inside the White House, where I got to meet him up close and personal, I became a complete loyalist. There would be no spying on his staff by me.

Even so, I leapt at the chance to enter the White House. I could have waited twenty more lifetimes before anyone else offered me a position as a writer for the president of the United States. Even a low-level writer. And there was always the possibility that Vice President Bush would lose the election to the Democratic nominee. What if this was my only chance to work in a White House?

Luckily for me, Bush campaign manager Lee Atwater and his

deputy, Ed Rogers, liked me, in sort of a sadistic, twisted way. Because of that "fondness" for me, they saw no reason whatsoever that I couldn't put in eight hours a day in the Reagan White House and then walk my tired butt over to the Bush campaign on Fifteenth Street to scribble into the wee hours of the night. No reason at all.

Contrary to what some in the mainstream media and some Democrats said about him, Lee Atwater had an exceptional political mind, was a bit of a Renaissance man, and was very spiritual.

As for Ed Rogers, he was and remains a class act and became a good friend and trusted advisor.

Of course, while I was doing both jobs, I had the brilliant idea that, because of my passion for spaceflight and as the twentieth anniversary of the Apollo 11 moon landing was approaching, now would be a perfect time to write a book about the twelve men who walked on the moon. I wanted to experience the most that life has to offer, and I had not yet experienced a complete nervous breakdown. Three tough jobs at the exact same time seemed like a surefire formula for success.

During this brief history of my time in 1987 and 1988, I also managed to forge a relationship with George W. Bush, which almost bordered on a friendship. Since George W. had his office across the hall from Lee Atwater and Ed Rogers, Lee and Ed would often park me in it when he was out of town or back in Texas. On more than one occasion, George W. walked in and found me sitting at his desk.

The first time this happened, I jumped up and apologized. He told me to sit down in his chair while he sat in a guest chair in front of his desk. During several conversations, he asked about my background and how I had come to work on his dad's campaign. I gave him a brief description of my childhood of poverty and my homelessness and the fact that I was often the only white kid in class.

George W. almost immediately began asking me if I thought the GOP was doing enough to reach out to black and Hispanic voters. I told him it was not. He then proceeded to tell me why the party had to do more, that it was not rocket science to get it done, and that for the party to grow and survive, we had to reach out.

Wow. Not nearly the rich-kid, Harvard-educated snot I'd been expecting. Not by a long shot. At forty years of age, George W. had turned a corner for the better in his own life and was quickly growing into a force to be reckoned with.

For whatever reasons, we bonded a bit. And because we did, George W. grew to ask for my help with more and more assignments.

It got to the point where he would call me at my desk at the White House or at home at night to check on the progress of the latest project he'd given me. All of the projects were totally on the up and up; even at that there was no doubting that George W. had a mischievous streak and a bit of Donald Segretti—of Watergate fame—in him.

He didn't have that troublemaker twinkle in his eye for nothing.

He was also very tough and *very* loyal to his dad. So much so that he was always thinking of ways to either protect his dad or weaken the competition. I actually admired his creativity and his devotion to family.

But, as alluded to, one or two of the assignments he gave me would not only be best if never carried out, but much better if never discovered by the media. One of those ideas was left on my home answering machine back in 1987.

Every once in a while, I'd play the tape to myself and laugh over and over again with the idea of it all. Clever, but crazy.

• • •

What I also didn't know about George W. in 1987—but was about to find out—was that he had a penchant for nicknaming people. Before I knew it, he had one for me. Mine was "Big Doug."

I was bigger than him in height and weight, but in truth, not by much. In 1987, I was six foot two and weighed about 205 pounds. George W., who was running regularly at that time, was six foot and a very solid 180 pounds. Not a small guy.

Regardless, that was the name he would call me forever more. Unfortunately, he'd also taken note of my accent. George W. got his MBA from a dinky little trade school up in Cambridge, Massachusetts, so he knew a good deal about Boston accents. My Boston accent was particularly thick since I hailed from Dorchester—as in the heart of Boston—so George W. was fond of asking me to say, "Park the car in the Harvard Yard."

So there are no doubts as to what kind of imbecile I was then and continue to be today. I truly had *no* idea why George W. or tens of other people in my life would ask me to repeat that stupid phrase over and over again. None.

Of course, when I would say it, it came out, "Pak the caaa in the Haaaaved Yaaaaad." True Bostonians like me don't pronounce our *r*'s. And not only that, we added *r*'s where they don't exist.

There is of course a logical reason for our very proper accent. Boston is the last bastion of civilization in the colonies that still speaks the King's English. Hence our lack or *r*'s among other things. Something the commoners should take into consideration before picking on us.

Since George W. didn't consider himself to be a "commoner," he delighted in asking me to say, "Park the car in the Harvard Yard." When I did, I would, of course, remove every *r* with the precision of a surgeon. To the contrary, if I said, "That's a good idea," it would actually come out, "That's a good i-deer." Proper English, I tell you.

• • •

Finally, without debating the often revisionist history and the pros and cons of the presidency of George W. Bush, I simply want to note that he is a very substantial person, a loving father and husband, and a true patriot. That's good enough for me.

29

Shedding Tears with the President

My first day walking the halls of the White House complex in my low-level position as a writer for President Ronald Reagan had me confused and almost overwhelmed with emotion. Every time I stopped to think about *actually being* in the White House, I was convinced that an old head injury had come back to haunt me and that I was surely hallucinating the entire experience.

At any second, I fully expected to wake up and find myself living in a car, on a park bench, or under a bridge somewhere. That's what happened to people like me. We never ended up in the White House stringing together words for the president of the United States.

And yet, as I continued down the halls, I was *still* in the White House. I was not homeless. I was not sleeping in a car, on a bench, or tending a campfire under a bridge. Somehow not only had I jumped through the magical looking glass, but those above me in the food chain at the White House—basically everyone—thought I was doing at least a passable job as a writer. Amazing.

Several weeks into the now-realized dream, I was sitting in my tiny cubicle in the Old Executive Office Building—part of the White House complex, and which houses 90 percent of the White

House staff—when the phone rang. I picked it up and identified myself. A second later, the voice on the other end of the line said, "Mr. MacKinnon. This is White House Signal calling. The president of the United States would like to speak with you."

Before the White House operator had gotten to the end of the sentence, I had already broken out in a cold sweat. *Why in the world is the president calling me,* I wondered. *Surely if I screwed up something, the White House wouldn't have the president call to fire me. Would they?*

One second after that ridiculous and paranoid thought, President Ronald Reagan got on the phone. As he began to speak, I tightened my grip on the handset as I felt it slipping from the waterfall I was creating in the palm of my left hand.

While most of the conversation was a blur, I do remember he thanked me for defending him in a recent column and asked if there was anything he could do for me.

While the public may not know or believe it, just because you work at the White House or even on the president's staff does not mean you ever get to meet him. At least not back then. Nowadays, all presidents host "holiday" parties. We live in a nation that is 80 percent Christian, yet even the White House—"the People's House"—refuses to say "Christmas," for cowardly reasons of political correctness. At these present-day "holiday" parties, the staff can get their photo taken in a lemming-like line that affords the staffer five seconds with the president. When I worked for President Reagan at the White House, lowly employees like me didn't always get that perk.

So, knowing this might be my one and only chance to meet the president, I screwed up my courage, closed my eyes, and stammered out, "Mr. President. I would be greatly honored to have a photo taken with you in the Oval Office one of these days."

As soon as I made the request, I expected not only the president to hang up on me, but also the Secret Service to bust into the room, grab me by the back of my sweaty neck, and drag me from the White House for being a rude little ingrate.

No, that did not happen. Instead, almost immediately, Ronald Reagan, the president of the United States, let out a quick chuckle and answered, "Of course. I'll have Kathy make the arrangements."

The reason the president was even wasting his time calling me was twofold. My job at the White House was to write presidential messages, surrogate speeches, and the occasional video speech. Two months into the job, I noticed that the president was getting blasted on almost a daily basis by, of all things, some alleged "conservatives."

What a bunch of ungrateful cretins, I thought. This guy single-handedly raises the Republican Party and the conservative movement from the ashes and *this* is how they pay him back? By attacking him because he didn't conform to their pencil-necked geek vision of conservatism.

"What's wrong with these people?" I muttered out loud as I read the latest in a growing line of "conservative" hit pieces against this extremely decent and accomplished statesman.

Even though I was a freshly minted and relatively young White House writer, I still had about one hundred columns under my belt with various newspapers around the country—an accomplishment that had helped land me the job—and I knew the process fairly well.

A column, I decided, would be the best way to get even with these "conservative" *traitors.* So, in an attempt to set the record straight, I sat in my cubicle in November 1987 and strung together about seven hundred words defending President Reagan against these mealymouthed ingrates, who in reality were just a bunch of untalented, socially retarded turbonerds who could only get publicity for themselves and their causes by attacking Reagan.

Once finished, I fired off the column to one of the few conservative papers in the country. This newspaper published it a week or so later, and a few days after that the White House operator dialed me up.

Before I knew it, my personal rendezvous with history had arrived. I was standing outside the door to the Oval Office, still sweating like Albert Brooks in the movie *Broadcast News* and wishing I hadn't been so bold.

Suddenly the door to the Oval Office swung open and a Presidential Protection Division agent from the United States Secret Service waved me in. As I walked in, the president stood up from behind his desk and walked toward me. We met in the middle of the Oval Office as the president greeted me with a warm smile and an extended right hand.

Everything seemed surreal and moved in slow motion. My knees felt more than a bit wobbly as the president's hand wrapped around mine. I could not believe that I was in the West Wing of the White House and had just entered the Oval Office by invitation of the president himself.

Didn't they know I was a nobody? Didn't they know I was one of the unwashed masses and not worth the time of the president?

The answer to that question was that they were most likely *very* aware of the nothing I was and my lowly station in life. And if they had their way, there was a better than even chance that I never would have gotten close to the Oval Office.

But fortunately for me, *they* were not on that special and magical phone call with me. Ronald Reagan was on the call, and he was about as far removed from *they* as any president could get. While not part of a particular church, Ronald Reagan was—like me—a very spiritual man who had a deep belief in Jesus Christ and His traditional teachings.

Knowing that, as I settled into the administration and had to wrestle with spiritual and political problems, I'd simply ask myself one of two questions: "What would Jesus do?" or "What would Ronald Reagan do?"

Ronald Reagan was not only a man of great faith, but at one time had been one of the "great unwashed masses." He never forgot where he came from and would never think not to figuratively and literally reach out a hand to those who most mattered to God. Even someone like me.

President Reagan was often kidded by the elites for wearing brown suits from time to time. He was also credited by others as being the "only man on earth who looked great in a brown suit." On this particular morning, the president looked more than dapper in his dark brown suit, crisp white French-cuff shirt, and soft red tie. Since red was his wife, Nancy's, favorite color, he enjoyed wearing red ties whenever possible.

The president's handshake was very firm, while his hand was soft and dry. Unfortunately for him, I instantly changed that. Just before walking into the Oval Office, I had uselessly wiped my palm one last time on my suit pant leg. By the time my hand rested in the president's, it had once again produced enough moisture to drown a small rat.

President Reagan paid no attention to my humidity problem but instead looked me straight in the eye, and with a twinkle in his, actually gave me his famous, "*Well . . .* it's nice to finally meet you, Doug."

Many times, when staff or outsiders enter the Oval Office for the first time, they comment later that it seemed "smaller than expected." At six foot two, I had an inch or two on the president, but even so, his stature, reputation, power, and warmness seemed to fill the room. I, and the most famous office in the world, shrunk by the second.

The president and I were not alone in the Oval Office. With us was that Presidential Protection Division agent from the Secret Service. As far as the Secret Service is concerned, just because you work in the White House and for the president doesn't mean you won't snap and try to kill him. So if that moment comes, they are there to kill you first. Also there was a White House photographer who was bathing the president and me in a constant wash of white light, as his strobe fired relentlessly.

While my subconscious was aware of these two other people

in the room, I barely knew they were there. The president of the United States is always larger than life and his—and hopefully *her* in the very near future—presence fills your consciousness to the point of overflow. As far as my mind's eye was concerned, it was just me and the president.

I looked down at the president's hand wrapped around mine and then back up at him and sheepishly said, "It's an honor to meet you, Mr. President. I hope I wasn't out of line asking for a photo."

The president kept his smile intact as he slowly shook his head, placed his hand on my back, and gently turned me to face the photographer.

After another flurry of photos and nonstop flashes that had my eyes seeing a bright white dot every time I blinked, the president turned back to look at me and his face got a bit more serious.

"Doug, I want to thank you for writing that column. Maybe some people think because it's the end of my second term, I don't matter anymore. I hope not. But regardless, it's nice to know that there are some young people like you out there who still think I do a few things right."

"More than some, Mr. President. There are millions of us out there who won't forget what you've done for this country and world. You're the role model for how all politicians should behave."

He tilted his head to the side, compressed his lips, and said a simple, "Well . . . thank you."

Just then, a door that led from the Oval Office to his assistant's office opened and I knew my time with the president was coming to a rapid close. I had rolled the dice to get here and was, at that very second, having a furious battle within my mind as to whether I should make the observation that was begging to get out.

As I did during the phone call, I decided to throw caution to the wind and just go for it. For all I knew this would be the first and last time I'd have a chance to have a real conversation with the president of the United States, and if my horrific childhood had taught me anything, it was that it's almost always better to ask for forgiveness than permission.

Having less than nothing can often reduce risk to a casual afterthought. What's the worst they could do to me? Certainly nothing worse than what I had experienced up until that moment.

Since working for President Reagan, I had come to learn that his father was basically the town drunk in Reagan's hometown of Dixon, Illinois. Ronald Reagan, his mother, and his brother were subjected to the usual taunts, insults, heartbreak, and desperation that come from living with a serious alcoholic. His dad was almost like Otis from the old *Andy Griffith Show,* and it tore him apart almost every day of his young life.

Knowing all of that background, I looked at the president, took a deep breath, and said, "Mr. President, I know I have to leave in a minute, but I wanted to take a moment to tell you that I understand how much you've overcome and what you've accomplished. My father has the same problem now that your dad did when you were a child, and I just felt it was important to tell you that."

There. I said it. I half expected the president to be offended with the comparison. Instead, it was as if for the first time during our brief visit, he took stock of who was standing before him. The smile left his face, his eyes seemed to narrow just a notch, and he stepped closer to me.

"How so?" he asked in almost a whisper.

I gave him a thirty-second history of my family life and the problems my dad and mom had with alcohol. By the time I was done, I was shocked and heartened to see tears in the eyes of the president of the United States. I could not believe it. Not only had I just said something that had real meaning to the president, but it was something that clearly reawakened in him some memories from his own troubled childhood.

Anyone who knows me knows that I cry during Pepsi commercials, so that was it for me. Once I saw the first tear in the president's eyes, I had to fight not to sob uncontrollably. Because this meeting was so personal and meaningful to me, the president's surprise emotion took things to a new and much higher level. As I felt tears run down my face, I was not in the least bit ashamed or embarrassed. All the opposite, in fact. I was in the presence of a man who not only got it . . . but who had lived it.

When you are the child of an alcoholic—or alcoholics in my case—you live your childhood behind a wall of invention, deception, and fear. You will go to the greatest lengths to ensure that your ugly little secret is not discovered by friends, classmates, or neighbors. At a very young age, you learn to "act" in order to stave off the dreaded humiliation that you know comes with exposure. As I looked at Ronald Reagan, I had no doubt he was thinking of exactly that humiliation, which is the constant companion of children of alcoholics.

As the president's face visibly softened and he and I both instantly dropped those protective shields, I wondered to myself what role his father's drinking played in his accomplished acting ability. Because of his childhood, I had no doubt that he, like Michael Caine, had begun to hone those skills at a very young age. It went with the territory.

With the kindest of empathy and caring, the president stepped even closer—as if to keep my secret safe and ensure he was out of earshot of the Secret Service agent, the photographer, and his assistant—and whispered yet again, "Children can be so cruel at times."

I sucked in my breath, became speechless, nodded my head, and held out my hand to say thank you and good-bye. I was not surprised when he gave me a quick hug. Such was the kindness and understanding of the man.

It was the rarest of moments with the rarest of people. A moment that helped me realize not only that such a background could be overcome, but that understanding and forgiveness had to be part of the process, if one wanted to truly move on and be in a position to help others facing the same pain and uncertainty.

This truth was reinforced to me by a president whose foot-prints I had staggered in, fallen from, returned to, and was trying to follow to the best of my ability.

And both of us were trying to follow the footprints and ex-ample that had been left for all of us to follow more than two thousand years earlier.

<u>30</u>

John F. Kennedy Jr.—
A Man and a Day to Remember

It is not every day that you get to meet "the best-looking man on the planet" and the son of our family hero at the same time and in the same person.

The day was May 19, 1999. I was director of communications for former senator Bob Dole, and the editors of *George* magazine had been calling me off and on for months asking if Senator Dole might come up to New York for an informal coffee with John F. Kennedy Jr. and the staff of *George*.

Because of my grandfather's connection to President Kennedy, I immediately thought it was a great idea, but the senator needed a bit of convincing. Not because he didn't want to meet with John Kennedy and the staff, but because he was not fond of going anywhere for just one event. If he was going to travel out of town, he wanted to make the most of his visit.

Since I really wanted to go, it was time to put on my thinking cap. The only way I was going to be able to engage John F. Kennedy Jr. in a conversation about his father and my grandfather was to figure out a way to fill up Senator Dole's schedule with New York City events. I instantly started making the necessary phone calls. With some work, and probably because the planets aligned a bit, I was able to fill the day.

During that time, Senator Dole was also chairman of the World War II Memorial committee. He and Fred Smith, the CEO of FedEx, were tasked with the difficult job of raising the massive amount of money needed to build this long-anticipated memorial.

Luck, the ever-invaluable persistence, and timing always play a role when things go your way, and it was no different then. In 1998, Steven Spielberg had made the Academy Award–winning film *Saving Private Ryan.* Tom Hanks was the star of that hugely popular film, which awakened a nation to the heroics of and the horrors experienced by the World War II generation.

About that same time, NBC News anchor Tom Brokaw—a truly classy individual—had published a new book that gave that generation a new name. He called them "the greatest generation." Tom had a chapter on Bob Dole in the book, which went on to be a huge bestseller.

After *Saving Private Ryan* came out, and as the World War II Memorial campaign was gaining steam, I joined a phone call between Senator Dole, Fred Smith, and Tom Hanks. The phone call was on speaker in the senator's office, and I was but a silent participant.

Because of the critical and box-office success of *Saving Private Ryan,* the movie's subject matter, and the high profile of Tom Hanks, it was decided that maybe Senator Dole and Fred Smith should reach out to Hanks to ask if he might serve as the spokesman for the memorial campaign.

No sooner did Dole and Smith start their pitch than Tom Hanks said, "I'm your man. What do you need me to do?"

On his own time and at some real sacrifice to his private schedule and private life, Hanks went on to film two public service announcements for the campaign and pitched in whenever and wherever needed. Politics aside, the campaign and the World War II vets were blessed to have him.

Just as they were blessed to have Fred Smith. In Smith—a decorated combat pilot who served with distinction during the Vietnam War—Senator Dole had found a kindred spirit who worked tirelessly night and day to raise the private funds needed to build this very moving memorial.

As I was moving the scheduling chess pieces, it turned out that Hanks was going to be in New York on May 19 to receive an award. Since John Kennedy and Tom Brokaw were based in New York, all that was required was some creativity to bring the moving pieces together so Senator Dole would venture up to the city that day.

The first part of the puzzle to put in place was calling the *Today* show to ask if they might want to interview both Hanks and Dole on the morning of May 19 to discuss the World War II Memorial. Yes, they would, came back their instant and enthusiastic answer.

Next I spoke with the editors of *George* to see if it would be possible for Senator Dole and myself to attend their "off the record" coffee with Kennedy and staff at around 10 A.M. "Yes it would," they said in response.

Last but not least, a fund-raising lunch for the World War II Memorial was to be held at the '21' club in New York at 12:30 P.M. That's right. The formerly poor, homeless urchin with dirt still caked under his fingernails was about to hang out at the ultra-famous and ultra-exclusive '21' club. Maybe Gordon Gekko would be seated next to me eating his steak tartare with a side of ethics.

The lunch was to be hosted by Senator Dole and Fred Smith, with special guests Tom Hanks, Tom Brokaw, and Katie Couric. The other invitees were some of the wealthiest people in and around New York City.

As a quick aside, it was at this lunch that I had a very up close and bizarre moment with Katie Couric. During the 1996 presidential campaign, there were a number of Dole supporters who felt she had stabbed both Bob and Elizabeth Dole in the back when she violated agreed-upon ground rules before a major interview. My feeling was that she had indeed been in violation of those ground rules, but since I was not the press person during that interview, I was not going to bring it up to her now. Furthermore, to bring up such a topic at an event honoring those who served in World War II would have been in bad taste.

At least, that was my opinion. Katie—whom I had known professionally for a number of years and whom, despite her far-left political beliefs, I always enjoyed speaking with—had different thoughts.

No sooner did she see me than she walked over to me, wrapped her arms around me, buried her head in my chest, and started crying about how bad she felt about that Dole interview from 1996. The only thing I could think to do was pat her gently on the back and tell her it was water long since under the bridge and not to worry about it.

She smiled up at me and through her tears said that while she was sure Bob Dole had forgiven her, she was not so sure about Elizabeth. I think she was correct on that score.

It was my understanding that Katie and her husband, Jay, may have been dealing with his health issues at that time. With that in mind, my first instinct is always to give someone the benefit of the doubt and as much understanding as possible. That's a courtesy that years later Katie did not extend to Sarah Palin or most conservatives.

Stress can and does affect different people in different ways. The tears and the strong embrace actually made her seem much more human and down-to-earth to me.

She quickly recovered and proceeded to light up the luncheon with her personality and energy.

• • •

So, that's how you fill a morning to get Bob Dole up to New York City to meet with John Kennedy.

Because Senator Dole and John Kennedy had never met before, I had asked the staff of *George* if it might be possible for the senator and John to meet privately for a few minutes first. They agreed, and the senator and I arrived at the magazine at about nine-thirty that morning.

We were instructed to take the elevator to the forty-first floor. Upon arriving there, we walked out into an empty hallway with some of the lights off. Just as the senator and I began to wonder if we had gotten off on the wrong floor, John Kennedy came around a corner and started to walk toward us.

As he stepped up to us, he apologized for being a bit late and then did something that few people do. He extended his left hand for the senator to shake. Many people don't know or remember that Senator Dole is disabled, that he lost the use of his right arm when severely wounded in battle in the hills of Italy during the closing days of World War II. For that reason, people who meet him for the first time understandably extend their right hand for him to shake, which makes for an awkward handshake.

John extended his left and the senator extended his, and they shook hands. John next turned to me and said, "Are you Doug? Nice to meet you in person." We had had one conversation on the phone prior to that morning, but this was the first time we actually met.

As I would later tell my wife, Andrea—and then she would have me retell her over and over again—John F. Kennedy Jr. was if anything even more handsome and larger-than-life in person. He made me and my fellow mortal males look like out-of-work trolls living under a bridge by comparison.

Looks notwithstanding, what impressed me most about John Kennedy was that he was a genuinely kind person. Over the years, I've developed a pretty good "I'm entitled" and "phony" detector, and it never went off with John Kennedy. Not once. In my opinion, what you saw was what you got. A humble, gifted, intelligent, and star-crossed human being who was determined to do some good with his life and the many gifts he had been given and developed during his time on earth.

John walked us down to his private office and asked if we wanted coffee. Both the senator and I said yes, and to my surprise, John went to get them himself. When he came back with the steaming coffee, we sat around this really cool round table—nothing to do with Camelot, I'm *almost* sure—and just talked about everything and nothing for a few minutes.

As we were wrapping up the conversation and preparing to head downstairs to meet with the rest of the staff, John stood up and motioned us over to one of the walls in his office. Once we were next to him, he proudly showed us a framed and matted piece of true American history. It was the actual signatures of every president from George Washington to, at the time, President Bill Clinton. Every real signature resting in its own square within the frame. John told the senator and me that it was one of his most treasured possessions and was a gift from his accomplished and stunning mother, Jacqueline Kennedy.

While my beloved possession may have paled in comparison to his, it still meant the world to me, and who better to show it to than John F. Kennedy Jr.?

As we were chatting and moving toward the door, I pulled the picture of my grandfather and John's father out of my inside suit coat pocket and showed it to him. Because he was an honestly good person, he seemed to take real interest in the picture and started asking me the expected questions. "When was it taken? Where was it taken?" That sort of thing.

It was one of those rare, wonderful generational moments in life. A generational moment in life with the only son of a president my grandfather had so deeply admired. A moment in life with a wonderful human being, who at the very least deserved a full life.

John further demonstrated what a considerate person he was after we got downstairs to the large conference room. Like all good staff members, as soon as I got into the room I immediately headed to a faraway corner, out of the line of fire.

The table in the conference room seated about thirty, with another forty or so chairs ringing the room. I went to sit in a chair in a remote corner of the room. Upon seeing this, John Kennedy walked over to me and asked that I come with him to sit at the table. I politely declined. He very politely insisted.

Thirty seconds later, I reluctantly plopped myself down next to John, with the senator sitting to my left at the head of the conference table. As it turned out, my proximity to John provided for some light moments and one fun but embarrassing episode for me.

During the course of the next hour or so, John would lean over to me and critique or comment about the questions being asked of the senator by his staff. Nothing serious. Just comments sometimes made with a glint of mischievous fun in his eyes. A glint that seemed to be there on a semipermanent basis.

The embarrassing part for me involved my watch. The day before, when I was leaving home for New York, I discovered that the batteries on my two "good" watches—meaning the ones that cost slightly more than fifty dollars—had run out. As I did not have time to get new batteries, I grabbed my twelve-dollar "runner's" watch. I liked it because it had a built-in stopwatch, which I actually did use when running. Unfortunately, it also looked like it had been sent through a garbage compactor several times. I don't think I can exaggerate how messed up the watch really was. It was supposed to be solid black, but was barely black because of the large gouges of white and silver from where I had bumped it and scraped it over the years.

The morning before, when I walked out of the bedroom, dressed in one of my handmade suits from Venezuela—very high quality but still a great bargain, since they were made by a dear friend of my mother-in-law—and looking, I thought, quite sharp, my wife's eyes went immediately to my wrist.

"Douglas. What is that?!"

I pretended ignorance. All men do this in the hopes of coming up with a clever response or dodge, and all men fail. As I was about to do.

"What's what, sweetie?"

"That thing on your wrist!"

"Oh, that's my runner's watch."

"Well it's disgusting. There is no way I'm going to let you go out of this house to meet the most handsome and debonair man in the world wearing that piece of junk. No way." I guess at this point I need to mention that my wife had long before made me promise that if John F. Kennedy Jr. was ever within sight of her, she could use my chest as a launching platform to leap onto him.

"But sweetie," I said smiling, "it's the only watch I have that works right now, and I'll need it to tell time in New York. I mean, you wouldn't want me to not *have* a watch and then somehow miss my appointment with the best-looking man in the world, would you?"

Ah-hah! I had created a serious conflict in her mind. She had become—quite rightly—the guardian of me not walking out of the house looking like a sloth, but she also wanted me to get to my meeting with John Kennedy, if for no other reason than so she could touch the hand that shook John's.

I could see her wheels spinning. *What to do? What to do?* Bing! She seemed to come up with a solution. I knew she would.

"All right. You can wear that monstrosity on one condition."

Conditions from her were always things to fear.

"What condition is that, sweetie?"

She walked over and grabbed the right cuff of my dress shirt and yanked it very hard to cover my watch. I was amazed the sleeve did not come off.

"The condition is that you promise, and I mean *promise,* that you will keep that awful thing covered up at all times when you are in the company of John Kennedy. It's really embarrassing, Douglas."

I sheepishly nodded in the affirmative and headed out the door to New York City.

As the questions kept coming, and as Senator Dole continued to make the staff laugh and applaud, my sixth sense alarm started to go off.

I'm no Obi-Wan Kenobi or anything like that, but I did feel the "Force" coming from my immediate right. My immediate right of course being where John Kennedy was sitting.

Senator Dole was talking to my left and everyone's attention was—or should have been—focused on him. As the senator was speaking, I slowly started to turn my head to the right. As it was swiveling, I noticed, to my horror, that the right sleeve of my suit and the right cuff of my white dress shirt had ridden way up my wrist. Not a good thing from a style point of view.

As my head continued its journey to the right, my eyes locked on John Kennedy's face. Alas, he was not looking at the senator as the senator spoke. No. Sadly, he was staring at the "unique" timepiece wrapped around my right wrist, the monstrosity I had promised Andrea I would keep hidden at all costs.

He stared at the watch for several more seconds and then realized I was looking at him. He raised his eyes from the *thing,* looked me square in the eyes, and with a very disarming smirk said, "Nice watch."

Busted.

After the meeting broke up, John and I walked out into the hallway together as Senator Dole spoke with the staff now surrounding him. As we did, we talked about the possibility of my doing some writing for *George*. I was deeply flattered that he would even consider me for his pages.

As John shook my hand and said good-bye and thanks, he did something very unexpected and touching. He asked if I might send him or bring him a copy of the photograph of his dad and my grandfather.

I promised that I would.

Two months later, our nation and the world lost him.

Tabloids, gossip, envy, and backstabbing staff aside, I am convinced that the United States—and especially the poor of our nation—are worse off because we lost that man. He accomplished great good during his short time on earth and would have gone on to do so much more. That was his being. That is who he was as a person.

31

The Secret Service Thinks I'm a Threat

For whatever reason, I'm mistaken at least twice a month in Washington for either a Secret Service agent or someone in a similar profession. My wife swore it was because I'm big, look mean, and never smile. She left out that on most days, my knuckles drag on the ground.

On this particular occasion, Senator Dole had agreed to be honorary cochairman of a fund-raising event for Washington mayor Tony Williams, along with then president Bill Clinton. The mayor, of course, was a Democrat. So when it was reported in the press that Bob Dole was going to attend and support a fundraiser for a Democratic mayor, we heard from more than a few upset Republicans.

"How dare you support a Democrat?" they all asked.

Senator Dole's answer, by email, or through me, was basically, "Grow up. Williams is a good man. He's trying to do the right thing for a city I happen to live in and which is in constant trouble; this town is never going to elect a Republican."

For years, Bob Dole was labeled the "hatchet man" for the GOP. But in reality he was one of the most pragmatic, reasonable, and bipartisan people in Congress.

It was June 2000. Senator Dole and I arrived at the swank home of Beth and Ron Dozoretz at about 5:30 P.M. Beth Dozoretz was a major donor for the Dems and a close friend of President Clinton. As for her husband, Ron—the guy with the money— Senator Dole and I were impressed to learn that he owned his own Citation X corporate jet. In our business, you never knew when you'd need a fast and luxurious ride.

At 5:30 P.M. the neighborhood was already locked down by the Secret Service. You had to go through several checkpoints just to get to the home of the Dozoretzes.

About ten of President Clinton's Presidential Protection Division agents—the ones who wear the suits and talk into their sleeves—were already at the home. The rest of the detail would arrive with President Clinton.

Senator Dole's driver, a wonderful man by the name of Wilbert Jones, let the senator and me off near the front of the house. They were expecting a hundred of the wealthiest people in and around Washington, including the likes of Steve Case of AOL and Bob Johnson of BET, so there were lots of limos and town cars lining the very upscale street.

Senator Dole walked up the path toward the front door, and I followed several steps behind. Ms. Dozoretz welcomed the senator at the front door, and he was immediately surrounded by guests who wanted a photo, wanted to shake his hand, or wanted to talk politics.

I followed him up the path at a respectful distance as I swiveled my head back and forth, taking in the luxurious surroundings as well as the positioning of all the Secret Service agents outside. Once inside, I stood off to the side of the foyer and proceeded to mind my own business. Five seconds later, a very large Secret Service agent walked up to me and introduced himself as the head of President Clinton's detail. We shook hands and I introduced myself. He then said something you don't normally hear every day. Or ever.

"Mr. MacKinnon, I need to have your weapon."

"Pardon me?" I asked.

"Your handgun, Mr. MacKinnon. I need it now, please. We can't have you armed when the president arrives."

I looked at him and shook my head. "I don't have a weapon."

"Aren't you Senator Dole's protection?"

Again, I shook my head. "No, sir. I'm just his director of communications."

You would think that would have done it. You and I might think that way, but this particular Secret Service agent didn't. It was his job *not* to think that way.

This time it was the agent who shook his head no. "No offense, Mr. MacKinnon. But we know you are Dole's protection, and we know you are armed."

This was getting stranger by the moment.

"Honestly, I'm not."

The agent then stepped closer and filled my field of vision. "Mr. MacKinnon. When you walked in here behind the senator, every agent outside started warning me about you in my earpiece. Every one. You've got the look, you've got the build, we watched you take in every detail as you walked behind Dole, and we know you are his protection. Did you once work with us?"

I know the agent was just doing his job, but geez. I pulled my business card out of my wallet, which identified me as director of communications for Bob Dole. Not good enough for the head of the president's detail. Nor should it have been.

The agent asked me to step into an empty room right off the foyer. Once there, he politely but firmly asked me to remove my suit coat.

I knew why, of course, but still said, "Why?"

"Because I need to confirm that you don't have a weapon."

I cooperated, and no weapon was found. Not quite good enough. And again, from his perspective, I had absolutely no issue with his thoroughness. The Secret Service can't afford to take anything on faith and gets no second chances.

Upon seeing no weapon on me, the head of the president's detail asked if I would consent to being patted down. As he asked, I noticed that another agent had stopped in the doorway of the small room and was now speaking into his sleeve.

I agreed to be patted down, and no weapon was found.

As I was putting my suit coat back on, the very gracious and professional agent shook his head one last time, leaned close to me, and whispered, "No matter what you say now, we both know you were once in the business."

I of course had not been, but I was not going to argue my case at the moment.

Unfortunately, the search and subsequent pat-down did not seem to allay the suspicions of the agent or his team. As soon as President Clinton showed up for the event, there was always at least one agent standing within arm's length of me as I mingled in the party. Especially when President Clinton and I stood off to the side and had a quick conversation.

I have *got* to start smiling more.

<u>32</u>

A Presidential Election
Hangs in the Balance . . . and
My Tiny Role in the Outcome

One of the reasons I was so anxious to go work for Bob Dole was that he was the senior statesman of the Republican Party, a certified war hero, and a true gentleman. And because I did end up working for him, I eventually found myself knee-deep in the Florida recount mess between then governor George W. Bush and Vice President Al Gore.

While I was a Republican when the recount took place in November and December of 2000, I am an *independent* conservative now and come down squarely on the side of traditional values.

I put no political party or person before my nation, my faith, or the welfare of those I love. While my beliefs of today often coincide with the stated beliefs of the GOP, the fact of the matter is that many Republican officials—like their Democratic counterparts—put themselves and party well before the interests and needs of our republic.

Understanding my strong disdain for this suicidal selfishness, what follows is written as best as can be remembered from inside the moment and with my then-GOP hat firmly atop my head.

•   •   •

As we all well remember from election day in November 2000, first the national news networks declared that Al Gore had won Florida and was most likely the next president of the United States. Then, several hours later, after a masterful berating by Karl Rove, which seriously helped turn the tide, these all-knowing, liberal-leaning, compromised networks reversed course and pulled Al Gore *out* of the winner's column from Florida. Several hours after that, they announced that Governor George W. Bush would be the next president of the United States.

Whoops. "Hold on," the networks quickly declared. "Maybe we got that one wrong as well."

As someone who has long-standing relationships with many in the media, including the national networks, I can tell you that without a doubt, most reporters and producers are very hardworking and try to do the best they can. Others, unfortunately, do their best only up until the moment when their liberal beliefs might be threatened. This was just such a time.

Another major problem with that business is that it is *very* competitive, and as such, sometimes the suits who run the networks strive to be *first* instead of *correct*. That explains the other major component that resulted in the train wreck of coverage that evening and for the next month or so. NBC anchor Tom Brokaw rightfully said, "We've all got egg on our faces," regarding the errors in reporting during election night of 2000.

Tom Brokaw—overall a very classy person and solid reporter— was correct. That said, he, like most of his colleagues in the business, would be hard-pressed to admit that blatant liberal bias played a major role in those errors and outright deceptions.

This bias manifested itself in two ways and had Bob Dole almost beside himself with anger and disbelief. The first was the tendency for some of the networks to "project" Al Gore the winner in a particular state when he was just barely up, by one or two points. The more damaging example of bias, at least as far as Bob Dole and I were concerned, was the networks' seemingly deliberate attempts *not* to declare George W. Bush the winner in states like Alabama, Georgia, and Virginia, where it was evident to all that he was going to win big.

Senator Dole's theory—which I agreed with—was that by adopting this strategy of projecting Al Gore the winner on flimsy numbers, as in Florida, and by withholding until the last possible second a projection of George W. Bush as a winner in states he was crushing Gore in, some at the networks were trying to create the impression that Al Gore was surely going to be the next president and that any voters for Bush might as well just stay home and not go to the polls.

In other words, they were *deliberately* trying to suppress the Bush vote. I would like to be able to suggest you go and ask today's "historians" about it, but the reality is that the vast majority of them—at least the ones the networks and cable networks interview on a regular basis—have a strong bias in favor of liberals and a far-left ideology. Talk about unethical and dishonest. A historian has a duty to have zero bias and simply follow and report the truth. Not to be a compromised flack. So much for that rule.

Don't forget that CNN and others projected Al Gore the winner in Florida while the polls were still open in the Panhandle of Florida and thousands of people were still trying to cast their votes. The networks claimed that even though the Panhandle was considered heavily in favor of Bush—and was *still* voting—they called the state early for Gore because of confusion over time zones and computer models. Not true.

On election night I had Bob Dole scheduled to do at least eight separate interviews with most of the broadcast and cable networks. During the day, I was in regular contact with the Bush campaign trying to get exit poll numbers to see how Bush was doing. I was being told that things were razor thin.

That night, Senator Dole, Mike Marshall, Dole's deputy director of communications at the time, and I headed out the door for the interviews with the networks. Because of the constant negative numbers and stories coming out on the TV news about Governor Bush and his chances, Senator Dole was concerned and slightly down in the dumps. He *really* wanted this one for Bush after eight years of Bill Clinton and Al Gore.

Whatever the real numbers were, a Bob Dole on national television with doubts would not be good for anyone on the GOP side. We and the Bush campaign needed him upbeat and positive.

In the car ride over, I sat behind Dole, who always sat in the front seat of his town car, next to his driver Wilbert Jones, so as not to appear like some "snob" riding around in a limo. For the entire ride to the first interview, I kept leaning forward and saying, "This thing is not over, Senator. Bush can still pull this out. The networks are fudging their numbers. None of this makes sense."

I said it so much it became like a mantra. Luckily, before Senator Dole got sick of my chant, we arrived at the first interview.

While the senator was still doing the first interview, I was calling the Bush campaign for updates and calling buddies at the networks for exit polls. For the first time that night, two things changed. My contacts at the Bush campaign sounded more upbeat, and my contacts at the networks sounded a bit more doubtful about some of their projections.

My contact at the Bush campaign told me, "Karl [Rove] says the the networks are one hundred percent wrong about Florida. Bush is going to win that."

By the time I had Senator Dole on the next network, uncertainty was filling the airwaves. By the time Bob Dole was at the third network and about two minutes from going on live, I saw Dan Rather—who would disgrace himself a few years later and basically end his career by using forged documents to go after then president George W. Bush—and CBS pull Florida out of the win column for Gore. *Whoa, baby. Time to get our game faces on.*

Dole was set to go on the air live in about twenty seconds when I basically burst into the interview room. The senator is not fond of swearing and does not like to hear it from his staff. But I had only twenty seconds to give him the news and the message.

"This is total bull----, Senator. The networks just pulled Gore out of the win column in Florida, and their projections are falling apart. There is a growing chance that Bush is going to win this thing. We *have* to convey that possibility to the voters the networks are trying to suppress."

Bob Dole is one of the best natural communicators in politics, and you didn't have to tell him twice. His mood instantly changed with the news, his eyes lit up, and he was ready to engage for Bush.

For the next four interviews, Governor Bush could not have had a better advocate or surrogate than Bob Dole. Let the record show that by the end of that strange night, Senator Dole was the first one to refer to "Governor" Bush as "President-elect" Bush.

Unfortunately for the nation, Wednesday morning came and with it the headlines "No Winner for President." The recount was on.

When the recount in Florida came, the Bush campaign turned to Bob Dole—and to a much lesser extent, me—for help. They turned to Dole because he was the senior statesman of the party—at least the senior one *not* related to Governor Bush—was a war hero, was respected by the American people, had been in this presidential arena three times, and had done such a great job on election night.

As for me, I had a number of friends at the Bush campaign, had done some writing for them, and had written some columns in favor of Governor Bush—including one in the *New York Times* where I recounted my relationship with him. That article caused a senior aide from the campaign bus to call me the day it ran and say, "Governor Bush is sitting next to me and wants to know how you pulled *that* one off."

So for the next five weeks, my life and the life of Bob Dole were a blur. So many people from the Bush campaign were calling me at home in the middle of the night that my wife threatened to move into the Hilton hotel down the street if I couldn't get the phone under control. I solved the problem by unplugging the phone in our bedroom so I could still take calls at two, three, or four in the morning in another room. Sleep, at that point, was highly overrated.

Aside from hitting Al Gore on television, the Bush campaign *really* wanted Senator Dole to hit Gore with columns in major newspapers. They wanted this because, more often than not, if you read about something in the *Washington Post* or *New York Times* today, you will most likely see it on the networks or your local news tomorrow.

The reason for that is twofold. First, some at the broadcast and cable networks tend to run a bit lazy and are more than happy to have others do the legwork for them. Second, and much more important, some editors, reporters, and anchors unethically took their marching orders from their liberal ideological masters at the *New York Times* and *Washington Post*. Hence a major reason to hit Vice President Gore in those papers. As it turned out, doing so had unintended consequences.

What we did was manage to upset President Clinton the very day we had to do an event with him.

As talked about, at this same time, Bob Dole was chairman of the World War II Memorial committee, and the *groundbreaking* for the memorial was scheduled to take place on the Washington Mall on Saturday, November 11, 2000 . . . just four days after the increasingly controversial election.

The groundbreaking was taking place just down the street from the White House and in the shadow of the Washington Monument. More than ten thousand people and veterans would show up for the historic event. The networks were all covering it and the guest speakers included Bob Dole, Tom Hanks and . . . President Clinton.

Privately, Senator Dole, Fred Smith, I, and many others had been hugely disappointed and even disgusted by the lack of support for the World War II Memorial from most Hollywood studios and executives.

Usually upon finally reaching a decision maker for one of these film studios—studios, mind you, which over the decades since World War II have made hundreds of millions of dollars in profit from World War II movies—the conversation from the executive's side was brief, rude, and went something like this:

Bob Dole: We are trying to build a memorial in Washington for our World War Two vets using private funds and at no expense to the taxpayer. Sadly, at this time, over one thousand World War Two vets per day are dying, so any immediate help would be greatly appreciated.

Studio executive: Well, that sounds like a nice project but it doesn't fit into our business plans at the moment so we are going to decline to make a donation.

Bob Dole: Really? That's ironic because World War Two didn't fit into *my* business plans at the time or the business plans of the over four hundred thousand Americans who lost their lives defending our nation while ensuring, among other things, that you could still make movies and a huge profit. Thanks for taking my call.

We were also told off the record by some in Hollywood that donations were not going to be made to the memorial because its chairman (Bob Dole) was a Republican.

Now, let's contrast that arrogance, ignorance, and selfishness with the incredible kindness, awareness, gratefulness, and sensitivity of director Steven Spielberg.

Besides raising money to build the memorial, we needed to raise a very healthy amount just to stage the groundbreaking ceremony, which would officially announce the construction of the project.

Months earlier, knowing we had exactly *zero* dollars raised for that purpose, I walked into Senator Dole's office and asked if he would mind if I reached out to Hollywood again.

He was understandably pessimistic but agreed to let me "waste my time if I wanted to."

Around this same time, I had struck up a relationship with one of Spielberg's top people and decided I had nothing to lose by calling him. His name was Andy Spahn and, like me, he had come out of the political world, although in his case, it was the liberal Democrat world. His and my politics aside, from the day I first spoke with him he was professional, classy, and always a man of his word.

I dialed Andy out at DreamWorks.

Once he was on the other end, I quickly went into my practiced pitch saying (begging) that if we could just get even one-eighth of the money needed for the groundbreaking ceremony, such a gift would be most generous indeed.

Andy stopped me in mid-spiel. "What's the entire amount you need for the groundbreaking ceremony?"

I was so used to hearing no and then a dial tone from these Hollywood types that I was shocked into confusion and my normal stupidity.

"Pardon me," I said. "If you mean how much would one-eighth of the amount needed to fund the project be—"

Andy stopped me again with a warm laugh. "No, Doug. I'm asking how much the entire project would cost. What's the full amount needed to fund the groundbreaking ceremony?"

I took a deep breath, let it out slowly and said, "The full amount needed for the ceremony is . . . six hundred and fifteen thousand dollars."

Andy thanked me for calling, said he would check with Mr. Spielberg and get back to me. True to his word, later that day he called me back.

"No problem," Andy said. "Steven says he will FedEx the full amount tomorrow. The World War Two Memorial is incredibly important to our nation and our history, and he wants you to know that we are proud to be a small part of it. Please let me know if we can help with anything else."

I was dumbstruck with that incredible and totally wonderful news. "Are you telling me that Mr. Spielberg is donating the entire six hundred and fifteen thousand dollars?"

"Yes. That's what I'm telling you."

Wow.

Two days later, a check for $615,000—in care of my attention—landed on my desk. I had never seen such an astronomical amount of money in a check before or since. Since it did say "in care of" me right on it, I quickly made a photocopy as a souvenir and then walked the check down to Senator Dole's office.

With one incredibly generous donation, Steven Spielberg helped to erase the pettiness and partisanship of a number of his Hollywood colleagues.

By a strange coincidence—the groundbreaking had been scheduled for *months,* so who knew we wouldn't have a president-elect?—the first column by Senator Dole basically stomping Al Gore, ran *that* very morning in the *Washington Post.*

The way the column thing worked was that I would coordinate with the Bush campaign on the content and timing. Three talented and overworked writers at the Bush campaign would come up with the first draft. It would then be my job to make sure it was—with the senator's strong input—written in "Dole-speak," and then place it in the *Post*.

Four days after the election, we wanted to tell Vice President Gore and the nation that this thing was over and that he had lost. We did just that in the body of the column and seemed to anger President Clinton just when we most needed him to shine at the all-important and *nonpartisan* groundbreaking for a memorial that was long overdue.

Senator Dole, Elizabeth Dole, Tom Hanks, Fred Smith of FedEx, his family, and I were all waiting in a tent next to the site. We were waiting for the president to arrive.

As another aside—and as a solemn reminder of our fragile and dangerous world—inside the tent with us were also several Secret Service agents and the "bat phone," or "red phone," or the "Hey, the poop has hit the fan and I've got to launch some nuclear missiles" phone. I did my best not to bump into it as I paced back and forth juggling multiple priorities.

Since President Clinton had a habit of being a bit tardy for events, we were all cooling our heels and making small talk. Twenty minutes or so after he was expected, the president walked in with his full Secret Service detail and staff members. One of those staff members was Doug Band. Currently Doug basically oversees all of former president Clinton's world and is someone I have gotten to know well over the years and consider a friend and class act.

To say that President Clinton was a bit chilly that morning to Senator Dole and even me would be an overstatement. But since this was President Clinton and he did genuinely like and have a great deal of respect for Senator Dole, he was soon his normal, engaging self.

After the event, I spoke with someone on Clinton's staff—not Doug Band—and got the scoop. The president had of course read the anti-Gore column by Dole first thing in the morning and he understandably was not thrilled with the timing. My friend said that the president also understood that it was politics and had a grudging respect that Dole had been chosen as the instrument to drop a hammer on Gore.

What follows is the collaborative column that ran that morning in the *Washington Post*.

DO THE RIGHT THING, MR. GORE
By Bob Dole (Used by permission)

It was a close election, but it's over.

Gerald Ford had narrowly lost his bid for the White House in 1976. A few changed votes in a couple of key states would have reversed the outcome. "Let's challenge it," many senior staffers urged the president. For others, it was a close call whether to demand a recount. But not for Gerald Ford. The quiet man from Grand Rapids would have none of it. He did not believe the country should have to go through a recount. America needed to get on with the business of setting up a new administration. We had already been through Watergate. It was time to set politics aside. It was time to let Jimmy Carter begin planning for the future. And like so many other times, Gerald Ford was right.

I was proud to be Gerald Ford's running mate in 1976. Proud to stand with such a good man. It took a while, but I was proud of Gerald Ford when he did the right thing by not contesting the election.

Twenty-four years later, America faces a similar situation. A close election has just been concluded with George W. Bush holding a narrow lead over Vice President Al Gore. Now, we have had two recounts confirming the governor's lead in the crucial state of Florida, but it seems the Gore campaign is choosing to ignore the clear precedent set by Richard Nixon in 1960 and Gerald Ford in 1976. Rather than bring the country together, they are making every effort to keep the nation divided for weeks with recounts, lawsuits and endless politicization of the election.

The American people deserve better. And the Gore campaign

knows it. As someone who could have become Vice President in 1976, I know first-hand how difficult it is to accept defeat. I urge Al Gore to put his country's agenda ahead of his agenda; to put the people's interests before his personal interests. There are several good reasons for that.

First, this is bad for the electoral process. America has just endured the longest presidential campaign in its history. In the old days, campaigns lasted a few months. Today, they last two years. And two years is enough. The American people have spoken.

Second, this is bad for the people. By dragging out the process the Gore campaign risks alienating even more Americans. Participation in our democracy continues to decline. More and more people are turned off by politics and are turning out of elections. It is precisely this type of politicization that continues to disenchant people. They want leadership, not lawsuits. They need someone committed to what is good for the country, not what is good for a post-election campaign.

Third, this is bad for the country. We need to get on with the business of the nation. The new president-elect must begin planning his administration. He must prepare a budget and begin selecting a cabinet. He must begin meeting with world leaders and a Congress already bitterly divided. A smooth transition will help to ensure a successful presidency and a more secure and prosperous nation for the next four years.

Finally, this is not good for Al Gore. History looks approvingly upon the examples set by Richard Nixon in 1960, Hubert Humphrey in 1968 and Gerald Ford in 1976. It will not look kindly on the first presidential candidate to challenge his election defeat in the courts. The presidency should be won through inspiration, not litigation.

I have served with Al Gore in the Senate. He is a good man who is on the verge of making a big mistake. One that will not serve him, his party or the country very well. Allowing the vote to stand may not be the easy thing to do, but it is the right thing to do.

Vice President Gore could allay the growing fears and cynicism by

clearly stating now that he will abide by the final Florida tally after all
foreign absentee ballots are counted, presumably on Friday, Nov. 17.

Senator Dole, the Bush campaign, and I next hit Vice President
Gore with columns in the *Wall Street Journal* and *Washington Times*.
We saved the final and best salvo for the *New York Times*.

My getting this column into the *New York Times* was considered
a real coup for the Bush campaign, both because the column would
run in one of the most liberal, anti-Republican papers in the country, and because I pulled it off with basically no notice to the *Times*.

The column was written, edited, and approved on the evening
of Sunday, November 26, 2000, and ran in the *Times* the *next*
morning. It was considered a minor miracle by all, and Senator
Dole and the campaign were never really sure how I pulled it off.

For me, it was easy. As stated, Republicans' first tendency with
any op-ed is to stay as far away from the *Times* as possible. The
usual reason: "They hate us, are left of liberal, and will never run
the column."

I disagreed. I told Senator Dole and the Bush campaign that
I had a very good working relationship with then op-ed editor
Katie Roberts, both because she had run one of my columns and
because she had run a column by Dole on the impeachment of
Bill Clinton, which I was heavily involved with. I knew Katie was
a straight shooter and might be very interested in this offering,
which she would instantly recognize as coming from the Bush
campaign through Bob Dole and myself.

Since the column was literally being drafted by Governor
Bush's speechwriters before going to Senator Dole for his input
and edits, I was begging the Bush campaign for a few minutes to
allow me to try to track down Katie, before we offered it to the
Washington Post or *Los Angeles Times*. Again, they thought I was
wasting my time but agreed to let me try.

It took a while, but I finally tracked down Katie at home and offered her the column. She knew it was news and that the campaign was making a statement and agreed immediately to take it. I'm not sure what happened after that at the *New York Times,* because the paper had been, as they say in the newspaper business, "put to bed for the night."

I was told later that they yanked someone else's column and squeezed Dole's in its place. What follows is that column:

WHY GORE SHOULD CONCEDE
By Bob Dole (Used by permission)

Four years ago, I conceded the presidential election as soon as the winner was determined. There was a lot less suspense that year than this time around. But when the outcome was clear, so was my duty.

Vice President Al Gore has waged a strong and determined campaign. But a narrow loss is still a loss—and for him, the moment to concede has come.

It arrived last night, when the Florida secretary of state certified that Governor George W. Bush had carried the state. The margin of victory is smaller than the electoral college itself, with its 538 electors. But the Constitution does not recognize near-victories. There can be only one winner, and one president.

Governor Bush prevailed in not one but four vote counts in Florida: the election night tally, the automatic recount, the count including absentee and overseas ballots, and now the final, certified total.

The vice president has been given a recount required by law, a hand recount in countries of his choosing, a generous time extension from the state supreme court, and almost every advantage that local canvassing boards could offer. The one thing he has not received is enough votes to win.

Now our country must receive something from him. He must have the good grace to accept defeat.

What is the alternative? We've already had glimpses of how a full and formal election contest would look. By inauguration day, January 20, the confusion, anger, and ill will of these past three weeks would be multiplied beyond anything this country has ever seen. It would be a courtroom circus on a staggering scale—a televised spectacle of legal ploys and power plays, carried, recapped and argued 24 hours a day.

The "contest" permitted under Florida law is, in fact, a lawsuit—a legal maneuver by the Vice President to overturn the certified result of Florida's election. There would be a trial with witnesses, examinations and cross-examinations, evidentiary rulings, motions, briefs—and of course, teams of lawyers. The first election of this new century would become the trial of the century—followed, inevitably, by appeals. Choose this path, and there is no going back.

The outcome of it all? Quite likely, the same result we have today—but with a nation even more divided and confused and embittered.

Never in our history has a presidential candidate filed suit to overturn an election he has lost, and for good reason: because the damage done would be far greater than any advantage gained. To their everlasting credit, unsuccessful candidates in all of our closest elections—most recently, Richard Nixon in 1960 and Gerald Ford in 1976—put the nation's interest ahead of their own.

I knew both these men, and trivia buffs may recall that I was President Ford's running mate in our contest with Jimmy Carter and Walter Mondale. We came just 30 electoral votes short of victory. But when President Ford was urged to contest the result in certain states, he wouldn't hear of it.

I know Al Gore, too, having served in the Senate with him and with his father years before. I well understand what he and his family must be feeling right now: defeat would seem like the end of long-held hopes and ambitions. But I am certain that he is able to rise above partisan anger and personal calculation, and I trust that he will.

It's been reported that on election night, an aide advised the vice president to "never surrender." In the drama of the moment, it was an understandable reaction. Three weeks and four counts later, they have seen it through. Yet what was once daring and defiant is now merely destructive. There is a transition to begin, a new administration to prepare, and to have a president we need a president-elect.

For Governor Bush, the reward is a chance to serve his country, and four years to build a legacy. For Vice President Gore, the chance to serve is now. He can spare our country a terrible ordeal and leave a legacy of honorable concern for the nation's good.

It should be noted that while Senator Dole said some fairly polite things about Vice President Gore in the previous two columns, in reality, he thought very little of Al Gore and considered him a "phony rich boy with no moral compass."

The incident that most troubled Senator Dole about Al Gore was one that came up during the Persian Gulf War of 1991. In fact, Senator Dole charged that then senator Al Gore tried in 1991 to trade his vote on the Iraq war resolution for a prime-time speaking slot during floor debate. Said Senator Dole at the time: "He was shopping, seeing where he could get the most prime time on television if he voted for or against the Gulf."

At it turned out, Gore was one of ten Democrats who broke ranks and supported the successful Republican vote to back President George H. W. Bush in going to war against Iraq to liberate Kuwait.

As Senator Dole has said, Al Gore "was looking to get maximum TV time in his quest to be on the ticket, and would vote with the Democrats against the war, if they gave him the time, or with the Republicans and for the president, if they gave him the exposure."

While there are a number of legitimate reasons for someone to have a less than charitable opinion of Al Gore, my reasons run a bit more personal. Especially one.

At the time of the Democratic convention in 1992, I found myself watching and then being offended as Vice President Gore used the near tragedy of his son being struck by a car as a cheap campaign prop during his speech.

Years later, the memory of those shameful remarks reentered my mind during the worst and most traumatizing episode of my life.

33

My Patrick

Every single day since January 17, 2001, I wonder what terrible things in a past life my brother, my sister, and I must have done to be continually and cruelly punished now. I especially wonder that for my sister, Janice. A more gentle and loving soul you could not find on the planet.

Throughout this book, I have outlined some of the pain and suffering I have endured. I have purposely left out some events and time periods that were just too painful to relive.

Even at that, if given the chance, I would beg God—as I have in prayer many times since—to revisit upon me *all* of that pain and suffering a hundredfold, if He would just take back a few fateful seconds or, at the very least, give me a few more seconds here on earth to be with my Patrick.

It was three days before the inauguration of George W. Bush as our forty-third president, and life for me—for a change—was heading in a very positive direction.

I had clawed my way out of poverty, had become a "success," and had accumulated enough money to look after those I loved for a very long time.

For the previous five years, my wife and I had had more downs than ups in our personal relationship, but I had been married to a woman who actually seemed to love me and wanted to protect me. I was moving toward more creative accomplishment in the book world, and I was blessed with wonderful relatives and friends. Finally, some peace of mind had come to my life.

On this fateful evening, my wife, Andrea, and I were scheduled to go to one of those coveted inaugural events leading up to the swearing-in of the new president at noon on January 20. This particular event was being held at the Corcoran art museum, just across the street from the White House complex on Seventeenth Street, and was going to be attended by the upper crust of Washington, D.C., and Texas. Some wanted to go for normal reasons. Others—the superficial especially—sought social climbing bonus points.

For that reason alone, I normally wouldn't go in a million years, but my wife had never been to one of these events and I wanted her to at least experience one in person. Hence I'd soon be climbing into a tuxedo, with Andrea showcasing a spectacular gown from Venezuela.

It was about six-twenty in the evening and already very dark outside. Senator Dole had gone home for the evening, and my co-worker and friend Mike Marshall and I were just standing outside our offices inside the Dole suite, shooting the breeze about politics, the crazy recount, and George W.

As we were doing this, I grabbed an old hockey stick I kept in my office and a rubber ball and started dribbling the ball around while I was talking to Mike.

About one minute later, something *instantly* happened to me that at the moment was unexplainable and very frightening. I was hit with the worst chill of my life. It started in my chest and then radiated throughout my entire body. As it hit me, my legs completely gave out. I backed into my office and collapsed into my chair.

Mike, of course, noticed what had just happened and ran over to ask if I was all right. I shook my head no as my hands started to tremble and my body continued to weaken. What worried me more than the physical sensations was the haze that seemed to be enveloping my mind. All this seemed to be happening in slow motion, and I had a growing sense of doom.

Obviously not sure what was happening to me or what to do, my first instinct was to call my wife at her office. Fortunately, she picked up the phone right away.

When she did, I told her what happened and asked her to come get me and take me to the hospital. She instantly started to fire questions at me that I had no answers for and then said it would take her a few minutes to get to me.

My right hand still trembled as I hung up the phone. As soon as I did, I started to feel guilty. My wife had never seen the pomp and circumstance of an inaugural event and I didn't want her to miss this one because of me. After debating the pros and cons in my clouded head for a minute or so, I called her back on her cell phone and flat-out lied. I told her I was feeling much better and that "maybe I had too much coffee today."

She was far from convinced by my explanation and continued to question me. However, like Michael Caine, my dysfunctional life had trained me to become a fairly decent actor when needed and after another minute or so, Andrea reluctantly accepted my story.

I asked her to meet me in thirty minutes near the museum, from where we would both head over together. A few minutes after hanging up, I started to feel moderately better, but still far from normal. Every sense of my being was telling me something was wrong. I just wanted to put in a quick appearance at this place and go home, take a hot shower, and get in my warm bed.

I walked with very uncertain steps to meet my wife at the agreed-upon place. As soon as she saw me, she jumped up off the bench she was waiting on and started to check me over. Once completed with her inspection, she asked with a small frown,

"Douglas, did you just lie to me on the phone? Because you don't look normal."

Still trying to keep up the pretense, I smiled back at my loving protector and said, "Sweetie, I feel fine. Really. Just too much caffeine today."

Since I didn't have any coffee or caffeine that day, I knew that wasn't the reason for my total collapse but I was still hoping Andrea would buy it.

She shook her head in response. "Then why are you so pale and why are your hands shaking?"

I smiled again. "Because that's what too much caffeine does to you. It gives you the jitters."

"Well," she said firmly, "I don't care what it is. I want to get you home."

I emphatically shook my head. "No way. You've never seen one of these events. You enjoy black-tie gatherings because they remind you of better times back in Caracas. And this is still a history-making and controversial election. So for all of those reasons and more, we are going."

She made one last attempt to dissuade me. "But you can't stand the type of people who go to these things."

I nodded my head. "You are right. I can't. But we are also going to a well-known art museum with spectacular paintings. I will concentrate on the amazing artwork on the walls and not on some of the guests trying to out-impress each other."

And so I did. The movie remake *The Thomas Crown Affair* had recently been in the theaters, and I remember joking with Andrea—as an ongoing homage to the master criminal path never taken—that I was just taking mental notes of the joint so I could come back later and liberate a Monet and a couple of Renoirs off the walls.

• • •

We left the museum at about eight-forty-five and started the fifteen-minute walk toward the Metro station near the museum. Just as we were about to enter the station, my cell phone rang. I was in no mood to speak with anyone, but I remembered that it might be Andrea's mom, who was visiting us from Venezuela, so I handed the phone to Andrea.

Andrea said a quick hello, and then her face instantly went dark. I knew something was wrong. My first thought was about my dad, who had gone into a hospital in Florida two weeks earlier. The doctor treating him—"incompetent" does not begin to describe how bad he was—had told us things were "touch-and-go." Because of my wife's face, I guessed I was about to get some very bad news concerning my father.

She hung up and I looked at her. "Is it my dad?"

She shook her head and said nothing.

"Well, what is it then?" I asked in a softer and much more worried voice.

I had never seen her look so sad and troubled. It was as if the blood was draining from her face as I stared at her. "I will tell you when we get home."

Starting to feel an anxiety attack building within me, I firmly shook my head no. Since I was a child, I always had to know instantly what terrible thing I was fighting and now was no different.

"Tell me now," I pleaded.

Her next seven words would all but destroy me and change my life forever:

"It's Patrick. He's been in an accident."

Patrick was my sister's nine-year-old son. He was—and is—everything to me. While he couldn't have had a more loving father than his dad, David, in my mind at least, no father could love his son more than I loved my Patrick. Emotionally, my ties to him were as strong as any father's to a son, and he was quite simply, as I always told him—and still tell him—"my best friend in the whole wide universe."

Because of all we had been through in our lives, I was especially close and protective of my sister, Janice. I was at the hospital with her and David the night Patrick was born. A night that was made even more special because our cousin Lillian helped deliver Patrick into this world on November 12, 1991.

Ten minutes after he was born, I was holding him in my arms. For the next four years of his life, I was with him every weekend. Playing, laughing, and causing trouble for his parents. Once I got married, I would have Patrick stay with us at least one weekend a month. He was the only source of true happiness and joy I had ever had in my entire life. The *only* source.

I looked at my wife on that cold sidewalk outside the Metro station.

"Is he gone?" I asked in a voice that was not my own.

She nodded her head and started to sob. While she was wrong at that moment, we did lose our Patrick three days later. In yet another cruel twist of fate—at least for someone who had been involved in the presidential campaign of George W. Bush—the doctors pronounced Patrick "gone" just as Bush was placing his hand on the Bible to be sworn in as president.

What I managed to piece together about the accident is that Patrick, along with two "friends," may have been running across—perhaps even back and forth across—a busy, very dark road about a half mile from his home.

After hearing various facts and hints, my initial belief was that Patrick was *dared* to run across this road in front of traffic by the two devious boys with him. My sister, Janice, insists that Patrick was way too strong mentally to be bullied and I certainly defer to her judgment.

Patrick was always small for his age, and whenever he would stay with us, he would tell me about these "friends" and others who would constantly pick on him because of his size. I always told him not to worry. His dad was a big guy, I was a big guy, and the men on both sides of his family were big. Just give it time. He would one day be big, too. That reassurance did not always stop his tears.

On the night of the accident, Patrick was wearing his dark-green winter jacket. The eighteen-year-old driver of the car never saw him in the darkness, until it was too late.

Again, while accepting my sister's explanation that Patrick was too mentally strong to be bullied, I still can't help but wonder from time to time.

I think about those two boys who were with my Patrick that night. They and only they know what really happened. What if they did dare him? One day, when they are adults, the gravity of what they may have done will occur to them. Because of who he is, I'm sure Patrick will forgive them.

Patrick is a much better person than me.

While I would never have had the strength to make the decision, Patrick's mom and dad—my sister, Janice, and her husband, David—courageously decided that Patrick's loss should not be in vain. Through organ donation, the lives of three children were instantly saved or improved. God bless them all.

Days later, I found the explanation for my physical collapse in my office. It turned out that Patrick's accident happened at *exactly* the same time I experienced the severe chills, body weakness, and collapse in my office. *Exactly.*

• • •

The day after we lost Patrick, we lost my dad.

When greeted with that news, I instantly asked God to explain to me the injustice and unfairness of this particularly cruel timing.

First, why did he allow a man who stole, cheated, abused and neglected his children chronically and purposefully, and destroyed all in his path, to live seventy-four years, but take a true angel on earth at nine years of age? Why?

Why couldn't God have taken just *one* year from my dad's wasted and selfish existence and given it to Patrick? If not one year, then why not one month, one week, or even one minute? Why?

Next, why take my dad at the *exact* moment all of our energy, focus, and faculties needed to be directed at dealing with the incomprehensible grief that was consuming our already waning sanity? Why?

When my brother, Jay, called me with the news, as he was down in Florida with my dad, I asked him to handle the necessary arrangements and have all of the bills sent to me. We would deal with my dad's passing when our minds could cope. And not a moment before.

Four days after we lost Patrick, we had his Mass.

The Mass took place at a Catholic church near my sister's home in Maryland. The Mass was held by Father Jay.

The *one* request my sister had for Father Jay was to make sure he pronounced Patrick's last name correctly. Patrick's full name is Patrick Ryan Ovide.

Time and again before the Mass, I told this priest that "Ovide" was pronounced "O-Vee-Dee." I even told him that an easy way to remember was to just repeat those three letters in the alphabet. O-V-D. Simple. Father Jay assured me he would not let my sister or us down.

Of course, during the Mass, the first chance he had to pronounce Patrick's last name, he messed it up . . . badly. Tears started streaming down my sister's face in disbelief, sadness, and anger. With her Patrick now beside her in the aisle of the church, this alleged man of God was inflicting even more pain. The *one* thing she wanted to go right had just gone terribly wrong.

I stood up in total disbelief and walked up to Father Jay and interrupted his worthless sermon. I leaned over to his ear and said, "It's O-Vee-Dee. Can you *please* get it right for my sister?"

Instead of being receptive or apologetic, he became visibly angry that I would dare interrupt his sermon. Right after I told him that and sat back down, he once again badly mispronounced Patrick's last name. At that point he had to have done it on purpose and out of spite. On the darkest day and at the darkest moment any parent could face, my sister had to be dealt this final cruelty by an uncaring person masquerading as a servant of God.

As for me, my personal pain that day was still to be compounded. I had written a very personal and uplifting story about Patrick in which I highlighted all the fun things and trouble we got into over the years. Upon getting to the church, I realized that I was in no state of mind to get up before those in attendance and read it. Not even close.

Knowing that, I asked a relative to read it for me *exactly* as written. He assured me he would. Once he got up to speak, unbelievably he decided on the spot that it was too long and gave his shortened and edited version of my most personal times with my Patrick. I was shocked and devastated by such an unthinking decision as the tears now rolled down my face.

As I had done many times in my life, I looked to my sister for comfort and support. She grabbed my hand as we suffered these final indignities together.

34

Am I Insane?

Am I insane?

Yup. You bet.

At least I certainly think so. While I may not meet some clinical definition of crazy, my mind has taken too much of a constant pounding over the years to be anything but scrambled and permanently damaged.

The lead-filled baseball bat to the back of my head that was Patrick's accident was the tipping point that started my irreversible slide into a place few people dwell.

So . . . knowing that, let's define one form of crazy. Up until Patrick's accident, I never thought that description would apply to me. Today I know better.

Before Patrick's accident, my definition of crazy was fairly rigid. Since the accident, that same definition has gained much more latitude and adopted a grayish hue. Define crazy. Well, for me, before the accident, it was anyone walking down the street talking to themselves. Today, years after the accident, I can't tell you how many times I've talked to myself in public—or at least, that's what a nervous passerby might think.

The fact of the matter is that I am talking to Patrick because I feel him with me. And because I *know* he is with me, I update him on his mom and dad, places we used to hang out, or a movie he'd want to see. Is that crazy? Some people would say yes. I certainly would have answered in the affirmative on January 19, 2001. Now I know better. Or at least I know enough to keep a very open mind.

How does the human mind cope with the loss of a child? With the loss of a best friend? How does it protect itself while it desperately fights to heal? Patrick's mom and dad, myself, and tens of thousands of people in indescribable and almost unbearable pain wish there were a blueprint. There is not.

As of now, no matter how much love and support are offered, you are mostly alone with your own inner demons in the guise of thoughts, questions, and doubts as you try to come to terms with "why?" Why my son, my daughter, or my nephew and best friend?

As mentioned earlier in the book, almost every day while at work, I try to take a long walk to clear my head and burn a few calories. Many times this walk takes me past the White House and then through Lafayette Park on the way back to my office. Recently, on my way back through the park, one of the very tame squirrels came up to me looking for food. Without hesitating for a second, I bent down, took a picture of Patrick out of my wallet, and "showed" him the squirrel. Is that crazy? I would have checked the "Oh, yeah" box before. But not now.

Now if I see someone doing something similar or anything out of the "norm," I don't jump to the conclusion that the person is crazy. Instead I immediately ask myself, *What kind of pain is that person going through? What kind of nightmare are they fighting alone? Who are they grieving for?* Not questions I would have asked myself prior to the accident.

Define crazy? My definition is an innocent nine-year-old boy being taken from this earth. What's yours?

. . .

In honor of Patrick, and as a way to help keep ourselves sane, we have created the Patrick Ryan Ovide (O-Vee-Dee) Foundation.

The idea for the foundation is to give out—free of charge— reflective stickers for children and adults to place on their jackets and clothing. I can't tell you how many times since Patrick's accident that I and others I know have come dangerously close, while driving, to a pedestrian in the dark who was running or walking across a street, far from the crosswalk.

There are thousands of Americans and tens of thousands of people around the world who are lost or injured after being struck by motor vehicles. It's a tired cliché, but if we can spare *one* life with these stickers and prevent *one* family from going through the ultimate emotional pain we've been through, then at least some good will come from the unconquerable pain of Patrick's accident.

For those who would like some information about Patrick's foundation, or even to donate, the address is as follows:

The Patrick Ryan Ovide Foundation
1141 NW 18th Ave
Boca Raton, FL 33486

35

Breathe and Count for Something

Wake up. Get up. Do something. Do anything. Every day after the accident, I repeated that mantra to myself as I continued to spiral downward. Don't let the accident win. Don't quit. Don't give up on life. Don't act on the dark thoughts that now fill your mind to the brim.

Don't.

Focus. Can you still be productive?

I think so.

How?

This. My life. My real-life experience. Surely it must count for something. If so, maybe I can make it count for somebody else.

What if I try to speak up now? Will anyone listen? Will anyone care?

Try. Please. Wake up. Get up. Do something. *Write* something. *Count* for something.

Howl at the moon if you must, but don't let Patrick's accident claim another victim.

Slowly, fitfully, incompletely, and between bouts of depression and crying, I tried to do something. I tried to stay busy. I tried to write something that would be relevant to people based on my background. In short, I tried to make my Patrick proud.

On May 21, 2002, I woke up, got up, and read a by-product of that effort. It was a column I had written for the *New York Times* titled "The Welfare Washington Doesn't Know." A column that spoke to the subject of poverty with some of my crazy life woven in.

I chose the left-of-center *Times* for several reasons, not the least of which was its massive readership and reach.

As it turned out, that one column brought me more public attention than at any point in my life. The attention was both wanted and most assuredly unwanted.

Mixed in with the wanted and unwanted were hundreds of emails and letters asking me to tell my story.

In the body of the column, I wrote of my life in poverty, asked members of Congress to imagine the reality of such a life, explained that innocent infants could not be held to blame for the actions of their parents or because they were born in a poor inner city instead of a wealthy suburb, and finally suggested that Congress actually have people who got themselves off the welfare roles come to Washington to testify both on how they did it and about the many obstacles they still face.

Though I had done a bit of television and radio in the past, I had never been so overwhelmed with requests. And they did not stop with the television and radio networks. My phone rang nonstop starting at about seven-thirty that morning, and my inbox was flooded with emails from well-wishers and people I had not heard from in years.

Clearly, the column had struck a chord, and I felt a responsibility to the subject matter to proceed cautiously and with integrity. I could have easily gone on every single show that asked me, but instead decided to go on just two programs: one network television program and one cable television program.

For the network show, I chose *This Week* on ABC, which at the time was hosted by Cokie Roberts and Sam Donaldson. As press secretary to former senator Bob Dole, I knew Sam and Cokie very well and had a great deal of respect for Cokie.

In trying to get me on the program, Cokie had picked up the phone herself and called. Not the usual practice among most of the talking heads with the walking egos. While certainly a liberal, Cokie was known as a fair-minded and smart journalist who understood politics and who had a good heart.

On the cable network side, I chose *Judith Regan Tonight* on the Fox network. I chose Judith for different reasons. She has always been someone I deeply admired. She is self-made, and has made it in a very tough business because of her brains, looks, and basic willingness to kick male executives in the nether region when needed. She had edge, and the subject matter needed edge.

When I appeared on the Sunday morning news program *This Week* with Cokie Roberts, to talk about welfare reform, a "misstatement" based on ignorance was made by one of the guests.

I was on the program that morning with then Republican congressman Clay Shaw of Florida. Shaw was one of the leaders of welfare reform in the House of Representatives and was and is a very decent person who honestly cares about the poor. He perhaps just needs to learn a bit more about the realities of poverty.

On the program, Cokie Roberts quoted from a Joyce Foundation study that listed the poverty line for a family of three living in the United States as being $14,750 per year. She then asked Clay Shaw if a family could be expected to survive on that amount.

The congressman's answer was "Yes. Of course."

Cokie and I were sitting together in the ABC News studio in Washington, D.C., with the congressman doing a remote from a studio in Florida. As soon as Shaw answered her question, Cokie looked at me, shook her head, and made a face of total disbelief. And rightfully so.

You can barely take care of your pet in this country on $14,000 per year, let alone a family of human beings.

Why would such a decent man like Clay Shaw say such a thing? Ignorance. An ignorance that makes him and others dangerously out of touch with the poverty-stricken men, women, and children of our nation.

I challenge those who don't know better to simply pick up any newspaper in any big city in this country and look up the lowest rents a family of three can be expected to pay. As of this writing, most of those rents hover well over the $1,000-per-month range. With many much higher.

So, after subtracting the rent money, Clay Shaw and others would expect and basically demand that this hypothetical family use the $2,000 or less they have for the *rest of the year* to feed themselves; clothe themselves; pay their utilities; pay for gasoline, public transportation, medical bills, and the many other unexpected expenses that make up life.

Maybe on the planet of out-of-touch, affluent people that's possible. But back here on good old planet Earth, such thinking is to consign fellow human beings to the slag heap of life and is totally unacceptable.

While nobody—and I mean *nobody*—is entitled to a free ride, I think it's crucial to remember that there are tens of thousands of our fellow citizens out there who are doing everything and anything to provide for themselves and their families and still can't rise above that poverty line.

Did my column and the talk show appearances do any good? I think so. At least for a moment. Did my words of warning and empathy reach a few of those most affected and troubled? I hope so.

Would I do it again?

Yes. I honestly think I have an obligation to speak out based on the ebbs and flows of my life.

36

WTP?

For me and the millions of people across the planet who had or have it much worse than me, a recurring question is "What's the point?"

For many of our fellow human beings in indescribable pain, it's natural to contemplate any and all ways to end such unbearable and unrelenting pain. Sometimes the black abyss just beyond the edge of the cliff looks like the answer. The *only* answer.

"What's the point?"

For some who are beaten down by the ravages of poverty and life, there is no point. Unless we can magically transpose ourselves into such people's horrific lives, then we have no business judging them. Sympathize, empathize, and help. But unless they commit crimes against civilized society, judge not.

As someone who has encountered some of the worst that life has to offer, I would only tell those standing at the edge of that abyss and considering the worst to step back as I did.

I would tell them—scream at them—that there *is* a point. There truly is. And that point, at least for me, is *faith*.

Earlier in my career, I was fortunate enough to interview all twelve men who walked on the moon. Almost every one of them proclaimed a deeper belief in God after seeing the Earth from afar and the cosmos from a perspective that only they and a select few have ever enjoyed.

I've also had the chance to discuss the beginning of the universe with a number of highly educated astronomers and scientists. Some are committed atheists.

They could—with the false confidence that springs from "educated" ignorance—trace the entire history of our universe back to a "spoonful of matter" and the millisecond after "the Big Bang" gave "life" to our universe.

These astronomers and scientists can speak for hours or days about that millisecond. But when I asked these incredibly intelligent scientists *where* that tiny "spoonful of matter" came from, they generally wrinkled their foreheads, shrugged their shoulders, and walked away without answering. The more honest among them said, "I have no idea."

You get that same reaction if you ask them how that tiny "spoonful of matter" could account for the uncountable zillions of tons of mass now in the universe. Sometimes the more we learn, the less we know. Unless, of course, you happen to be a compromised scientist pushing a specific agenda.

There is a growing cottage industry within liberal publishing that is teeming with liberal and "unbiased" scientists and commentators out to prove that God does not exist. Fine. Other than arrogance from ignorance, I'm hard-pressed to explain why the existence of God scares them so.

They are certainly entitled to their beliefs, as long as they don't attack, belittle, or ridicule others while fabricating "science" to prop up their atheist views. While I believe there are much more urgent issues to be solved in our world with their time and our precious and limited resources, I don't pretend to understand the liberal mind-set.

One thing I do know is that most of these liberal scientists and commentators who are working overtime to disprove the existence of God come from privileged and wealthy backgrounds. While I don't begrudge them that elite status, I do think that their overall understanding of life is viewed through a tiny and clouded prism that allows in only a fraction of the illumination needed for rational thought, understanding, and the confidence to admit that they understand much less than they think they know.

I ultimately feel very sorry for those who lack faith. Faith not only in God, but faith in the Golden Rule, faith in the rule of law, and faith in the goodness that is embedded within the souls of most on this planet.

We all tend to do better in life if we have someone we don't want to disappoint. Someone we don't want to let down.

For me at a very young age, that "person" became my Baby Jesus. Often He, through my cheap plastic little Nativity scene, became my only counsel and confidant. As I grew older, I became more spiritual, and His simple teachings of love, peace, and sacrifice resonated more and more.

Today I have friends who are Christians, Roman Catholics, Jews, Muslims, Buddhists, and nonbelievers. Each came to their beliefs and faith—or lack thereof—through life experience.

While I respect all and appreciate their varied life experiences, I happen to be a Christian who believes that God does not welcome one faith while condemning another. We are *all* his children, and we should *all* be equal in His eyes if we obey His rules and the rules of law.

So, while I am not a fan of "organized" religion—or at least many of the "leaders" of organized religion—I do respect those who are.

No matter whether we are "organized" or not, if we have the faith liberal scientists lack, then we truly do believe—and know—that there is life after life. But to get there, we have to put our faith in God and be the best we can possibly be here on earth . . . even when we think no one is looking.

• • •

Obviously, life can indeed be cruel. Much crueler for some than for others. But for me life is still an adventure. It is still the only game in town until we reach that next level.

With all that my sister, my brother, and I have been through, I still believe that life is incredible. I am still fascinated with the possibilities and mysteries a new day will bring. We have been given a wonderful planet with wonderful people. It's up to us to find the very good among the oftentimes very bad and make something positive come from the discovery and the relationships.

Some have criticized me for only seeing life in terms of black-and-white. They may have a point. But it is also a point made by people who have *never* experienced the kind of pain I and millions of others have gone through. Seeing things in terms of black-and-white is just one more way of protecting your mind and easing or eliminating pain.

For me, life *is* black-and-white. We can complicate it, but it's really a very simple proposition. If we are lucky, we are going to get about eight decades on the planet. What are we going to do with those eighty years? What are we going to do with that gift? How can we help others and ourselves along the way?

Every day when I was poor, I would wake up and wonder how I could try to improve my life. In a strange way, I relished the challenge that life was throwing at me. The constant fight and struggle at least gave me a constant purpose.

But what I also learned at that early age was that I didn't have to play by life's rules. I could and did invent my own. When you are poor, you can't have the rules dictated to you by the rich, by the pampered, or by the ignorant, no matter how well-intentioned they may be.

At certain times you need to invent your *own* rules for life. I did. Sometimes I was right. Sometimes I was wrong. Sometimes I moved forward. Sometimes I slid further backward.

But with each decision, each movement, and each result, I knew, based on my beliefs, my experience, and my faith that I had done the best I could with what I had.

A lot of things have gone wrong in my life, but I still seek out the good and the positives. The positives for me are my family, my friends, and my faith.

Out of all these positives stand my sister, Janice, and my brother, Jay. My childhood was *their* childhood. My pain and suffering was *their* pain and suffering. My childhood story is *their* childhood story.

Somewhere along the way during that childhood, Jay and I chose radically different paths. That's okay.

While he may have stumbled in the footsteps of our father for a while, he has been on the right track for twenty years now, and I am so very proud of him. You cannot find a person with a better heart than Jay.

As is no doubt evident in these pages, the biggest positive from my childhood was my "big" sister Janice. Today, after all of her loss and pain, she remains one of the most gentle, loving, and giving people on the planet. She is a remarkable woman.

Another positive in my life came in the form of an unintended gift from my sister several years before the gift of Patrick. Janice, like many girls in poverty, got pregnant at a young age. She was not married but had a wonderful daughter named Christina. As with Patrick, I got to play a significant role in Chrissy's early years.

While Chrissy unfortunately was later both forced into and created a great deal of dysfunction on her own, she is making steady progress and remains—as a single mom herself—a large part of my life and someone I dearly and unconditionally love. We have an unbreakable bond and she is one of the few (along with my sister) who understands that I never had a childhood to speak of and encourages my inner child to sneak out as much as possible.

Before my sister's husband, David, met and married her, he had a young daughter named Julie. David was a single dad when he met Janice, and after the wedding, Julie and Chrissy became sisters. That was trouble. Fortunately, we had Patrick to rat them out on a regular basis.

Julie is also someone who created unnecessary dysfunction when younger but now works extremely hard to be a better mom, provider, and person. She is doing a fantastic job.

As for the extended immediate family, I would be remiss if I did not mention my aunt Mary. She was my dad's sister, the only girl among six brothers, and over the years became like a second mom to us, especially to me and Janice. She is a wonderful and very spiritual woman who brings a smile and joy to everyone she meets.

Finally, my wife has had my back in many ways over the years. That said, between the issues she brought into our marriage, my obvious lifetime of drama, and our shared tragedies, we continue to have our ups and downs. Sadly, the downs seem to be winning at the moment and as of this writing, we have separated. Again . . . that life-*really*-hurts thing.

No matter. To complete the circle of this story and this book, one of the things I will be most grateful to Andrea for is that she helped to bring my dad back into my life. From the age of seventeen on, I barely talked to him or acknowledged his existence. In the eight years prior to meeting Andrea, I had not seen him or spoken one word to him.

Andrea is very close to her mom and was especially close to her beloved dad, Paul. Thus she started to insist that I at least pick up the phone and say hi to my father. Partly to stop her from asking and partly because what she was saying was starting to make some sense to me—*forgiveness* and all of that—I did just that. I called my father, John, and had a tentative but polite conversation.

That conversation took place in April 1994, right around his birthday. From then on I called him once a month, then twice a month, then once a week, then several times a week. My dad lived down near Jay in Florida at this point, and by coincidence, Andrea's mom had a condo about thirty minutes away from my dad.

I visited him about two or three times a year after that initial phone call and made him part of my wedding party when Andrea and I got married. To this day, the best Thanksgiving I have ever had was the one Andrea and I had with my dad in Florida in 1999. It was just the three of us, and everything worked out wonderfully.

My dad and I never talked about the past or the tremendous pain he caused us and others, and that was okay with me. He had found a level to his drinking and was an extremely bright man, still intellectually curious, and great company.

I was last with him on Christmas Day of 2000. My dad told me that the best gift he could possibly have had was me coming to visit him.

His saying that became my very meaningful and precious Christmas present, which no one could ever take away.

PART TWO

A Message

I want to turn from the story of my life to a few of the lessons and realities that life taught me. Obviously, those lessons, realities, and even messages grow out of my experiences as a child living in abject poverty, constant ridicule, and very few options. In other words, that real-life thing again. Equally important to my perspective are the opportunities I have created and seen in my adult life—proving that with hard work, personal responsibility, and faith, it is possible to get out of the cycle of poverty and even one day be in a position to actually help others. That said, what follows are some of those lessons, realities, and messages.

1

Poverty Is Not Partisan

The understanding and empathy that Ronald Reagan learned as the child of an alcoholic—and that years later was purposely twisted by unethical elements of our media—is that poverty is not a state of mind. It's real. It's relentless. It's cruel.

And if you don't figure a way out, it will eventually defeat you. It will defeat you mentally. It will defeat you physically. And then, finally, when you think you can take no more, poverty will gleefully lead you to the edge of the abyss and dare you to jump. Tragically, many do.

Some jump in the literal sense, where suicide becomes a way out for many human beings who bend, bend, bend and then finally break under the pressure of the latest and final indignity forced upon them by circumstances often totally out of their control. If you have not suffered through true, relentless, abject poverty, you have no idea—none—of the despair, hopelessness, and constant pain that assaults every sense of your being as you struggle to survive. As you struggle just to breathe.

For the most part, however, when I say jump, I mean that poverty dares you to jump into the easy way out. To jump into the bottle. Jump into drugs. Jump into crime. Or jump into a lifetime of excuses.

Poverty never dares you to jump to safety, jump into school, jump into faith, or jump into the arms of those who may protect you. Poverty only leads you to that bottomless dark hole for one reason . . . to propel you over the edge to your final fall.

Sympathize, empathize, and imagine. But thank God, thank your parents, and even thank yourself if you've never had to experience what millions upon millions of your fellow human beings try to escape every day of their lives . . . and most fail in the attempt.

One of the ironies of my "success" is that I don't, and never will, consider myself rich. While monetarily I'm now very well-off, my mind-set is still that of someone who had to exist on vapors for all of my formative years.

I went through and survived something the vast majority of Americans will never know, understand, or defeat. And because of that, for better or worse, I've got a wealth of knowledge on poverty, crime, and human nature that most in politics . . . or life . . . will never have. Given a choice, I would have much preferred to grow up in a middle- or upper-middle-class environment where I never would have learned the lessons taught by severe poverty, but since I didn't, it seems right to do something useful with my unique knowledge base.

Coming from that environment, it would be fair to say that I'm disappointed and saddened to see so many people who have the blessings of wealth and a "functional" family, yet ignorantly wallow in those blessings as they board the SS *Hedonism* for another trip to the Caribbean, Europe, and all points rich. All the while pretending that poor people don't exist, or that if they do, they are lazy, criminals, and minorities and are getting what they deserve.

One of the problems and, in fact, dangers, is that there are a number of people in Congress and the administration who actually believe that. And I'm talking *any* Congress and *any* administration. Poverty truly is not—and cannot be—a partisan issue.

Republican or Democrat, there are far too many people making laws that affect the lives of truly poor Americans but who have zero idea what they are talking about or what life is like for Americans living below the poverty line. They were born into money, made a great deal of money, or just plain forgot where they came from. Regardless, their ignorance and unwillingness to learn or help makes them the enemy of those trying to escape poverty.

What these ignorant members of Congress know about poverty or the pain of those suffering silently in its clutches can be written on the head of a pin, with room left over for the contents of the New York City phone book.

As to why many of our elected officials really don't care about the poor, the answer is very simple. The poor don't vote. And if they don't vote, they don't exist for these politicians. It's that basic and that sad.

It's precisely because of that harsh reality that the poor of our nation need to understand that if properly exercised, their votes can and will count. And with those votes comes power. And with that power they will strike a degree of fear in the gutless and disrespectful politicians who refuse to give the poor their due.

If the poor learn to vote as one on certain issues that will empower our traditional values—and therefore themselves—they will instantly vault to the status of one of the most powerful and respected voting blocs in the nation.

Unfortunately, that is a lesson most in poverty have yet to comprehend and a tool most have yet to utilize.

2

Poverty's Unsung Heroes

When I worked for former senator Bob Dole as his director of communications, one of the things he repeatedly stressed to me was that he thought the word *hero* was thrown around much too loosely in this country. I could not agree more.

Senator Dole basically left his right arm and three years of his life on a hilltop in Italy defending freedom, and in my opinion has earned the right to define the word *hero*. A title, by the way, he never claimed for himself.

Today, we foolishly call athletes, rap artists, actors, "reality stars," and just about anyone else who doesn't deserve the title *hero*. They are many things, but hero is certainly not one.

I'd like to nominate an entire group as the all-time heroes. A nomination that may upset some of my fellow conservatives or some who claim to speak for Jesus or their particular faith.

The group I'd like to nominate is *single mothers*.

If you are a follower of Jesus or if you are a person of true faith, then remember that Jesus once said, "Let he who is without sin cast the first stone" (John 8:7).

Did many of these single mothers—like my sister years ago or my niece now—allow themselves to be used or to cross lines that should never have been crossed? Absolutely. Should they and their precious children now be punished for a mistake or because the "men" in their lives abandoned them? Of course not.

And yet it happens every day in our society. Many people—even people of "faith"—look down their noses at these women, or worse, turn their backs on them.

While pregnancy out of wedlock is much more prevalent among the poor, it happens quite frequently among the rich as well. But the rich can send their pregnant daughters to "school" in Switzerland for a year until they give birth and put the baby up for adoption. In other words, the pregnancy and the birth never happened, and the reputation of their daughter is intact.

And poor or rich, if you do choose to keep your baby and not succumb to the vile alternative of ending a viable human life, then you are especially to be commended and protected.

Sadly, such protection and acknowledgment mostly attaches to the wealthy. If you are desperately poor and still choose to keep your baby, you are often called the worst of names and abandoned in the process. Why?

My life has been nothing if not "real-life" experience. No academic mumbo jumbo and no useless white papers written by academics out to impress each other at the expense of the truly needy.

No. On the subject of helping single mothers, my knowledge is gained from being deeply involved in the process as I sought first to help my sister, and years later, my niece Chrissy.

My niece, who became pregnant at nineteen, offers one example out of many. While pregnant, she was offered help and counseling, but after her son was born, she has not been offered help even once. Not once.

In this case, it was the Catholic Church that offered help while she was pregnant. To be sure, the church excels at doing anything and everything possible to make sure young girls and women don't abort the life inside of them. And for that they should be applauded and thanked.

But when the child is actually born, the Catholic Church—at least in our experience—is missing in action. For those in the church whom we dealt with, it seemed as if their mission was accomplished once my niece gave birth. After that, she and her infant son were on their own.

Mistakes happen. Unwed young girls and young women get pregnant. Many face rejection from their families, from their friends, from their schools, and from the "safety net" that was created to help them in their time of need.

No one should ever want or encourage a birth out of wedlock. For a child to develop properly, he or she needs both a mother *and a father* in his or her young life. Period. And a *married* mother and father at that.

But, as they say, "life happens while you are making plans." And when life does happen—in this case the pregnancy of a young girl or woman—then the darker side of life also often happens. Abandonment on all fronts. Especially for those struggling below the poverty line.

For whatever reasons—and of course these young women often bear personal responsibility—these women are now single mothers and very well may remain single mothers for the rest of their lives.

Leaving aside the false and insulting clichés of bad movies, what those who abandon these young women don't understand is that for the most part, these single moms then go out and do everything within their power to provide for the young life or lives they bring into the world.

They work anywhere from one to three generally low-paying, backbreaking jobs. They do this as they pay the bills, teach their children right from wrong, wash the clothes, shop for food, clean the house, barely get any sleep, have no life of their own, and then start the entire thankless process all over again in the morning. All, mind you, with very little or no support.

While they are not athletes, rap "stars," or actors, if you want to see a real American hero, search out a responsible single mom who day in and day out is struggling to do the right thing. A woman who courageously did not end a viable life, who did not turn her back on her responsibility, and who—at great sacrifice to herself—is raising her child or children to the best of her ability.

Other than His Son, God does not make perfect people, but He did personify extraordinary decency, extraordinary effort, and extraordinary love.

Seek out one of these single moms. And in the process, see if you can help. We are our brothers' *and sisters'* keepers.

3

Poverty—A Ready-Made Excuse
for the Weak of Mind and Faith

Let me see if I understand this correctly. If you were born into a life of poverty and despair, you have no choice but to rob, murder, rape, drink, use drugs, not work, game the system, and never, ever accept responsibility for your actions.

One of the tragic by-products of poverty is excuses. In my estimation it is by far *the* most destructive by-product.

As one who witnessed some use poverty as a crutch or rationale for why they did irrational, bad, or even evil things—or nothing at all—I've truly grown to hate the phrase "I did [name the crime] because I'm poor, a minority, I have no chance to escape, and the world owes me a living."

Well, you know what? To those who live in poverty and try to justify the horror they visit upon their fellow human beings—or even themselves—because of that poverty, I only have this to say: "You only bring shame to yourselves and your families."

Going without is hard, but maintaining your morals, dignity, integrity, and character in the face of such despair is even harder. It's harder, and yet it's done millions of times a day by millions of people around the world who fight to feed their children, pay the rent, and go to work. They endure this struggle, but refuse, in the midst of a sometimes unwinnable battle, to take the easy way out.

In my opinion, they do so because faith plays a critical role in their decision-making process. Faith in God, and faith in themselves. And from that they gain the wisdom to understand that taking and exercising personal responsibility is paramount in the never-ending fight against poverty or the injustices of life.

As someone who was fortunate enough to escape poverty, find some professional success, and work in the government and with the media along the way, I have a finger or two of blame to point at the guilty.

The first finger is pointed straight at the media. Why are some in that profession fixated upon showcasing those who have fallen into crime, drugs, or booze—almost always a vapid TV or movie celebrity, but *never* showcasing or highlighting those who had the strength *not* to fall into that trap in the first place? Where's *that* story? Where's *that* person?

Why can't the media find these Americans struggling to make it to the next day in *any* of our inner cities or rural areas and get their stories on the air? How costly would it be for them to air the story of a good, hardworking, decent, but *unknown* poverty-stricken American, instead of the "flavor of the month" celebrity who got bored with the money, the mansion, the Gulfstream V, and the adoring fans, and fell into a habit of cocaine and anorexia. Disney "stars," anyone?

The mainstream media could very easily air or print the stories of those who work two and three jobs to feed their children, pay the rent, and try to do the right thing. Just as they could expose the public school system—especially inner-city public schools and teachers' unions—as woefully inept, corrupt, and failing their students.

But because most employees at the networks are liberal, and one of the sacred cows of the liberal movement is bad teachers and corrupt teachers' unions, the networks choose to look the other way and let the children suffer. Bottom-feeders with a bias.

Tragically, while the television networks commit this crime against the poor, another part of the "entertainment" community works overtime to exploit these very same true American heroes and their children.

This side of the entertainment community deliberately targets "at risk" African-American and Hispanic-American children. Both white and minority entertainment executives willingly poison the minds of these young kids—kids who hover at or below the poverty line—for one reason and one reason only: the almighty dollar.

These minority entertainment executives pimp young minority recording artists, whom they then train to exploit young, impressionable minds, take the little money these young fans have, and then use it to fund their immoral, materialistic lifestyles. They do this while putting out some of the most demeaning and destructive lyrics ever heard. Most of those vile and criminal lyrics are directed at minority women.

Writer P. J. O'Rourke once rightfully referred to them as Poverty Pests: a class of subhumans who basically owe their entire employment existence and often extreme wealth to the misfortune of others. They effectively prove that society never lacks for those who will use any situation for their own gain. The poor have always presented a most inviting target for this kind of person, and it's up to all of us to scream, "Enough is enough!"

A large part of the Poverty Pest club is academics. Many are destructively ignorant fools who exist atop ivory towers—I say exist, because they have never "lived" the lives they write about—and make the lives of the poor more hopeless and difficult because of their idiotic pronouncements.

When did real-life talent and experience come in a poor second place to ivory tower pronouncements and egos? The answer, it seems, is forever.

With regard to talent and experience, I have a theory that I would like to put forward. While I don't think this theory is original to me, I seem to say it to people an awful lot.

I call it the 20-60-20 rule. In *any* profession, be it politics, journalism, academics, car-making, whatever, the 20-60-20 rule applies. On any given day at any given place of employment, 20 percent of the people who work there are incredibly responsible and will always strive to do their best and get the job done. They may not want to be that responsible, but they have an inner voice that tells them, "If not you, who? If you don't do it, it's not going to get done and bad things are going to happen." So, often at great cost to themselves, they *still* get the job done.

Next comes the 60 percent in the middle. They don't want to do anything bad, but they also don't necessarily want to do anything good. They just want to get by, put in their eight hours a day, and be unnoticed. They straddle the fence of indifference and really like it up there. Success to them is to put in thirty years, grab one of those fat, unfunded pensions that's sweetened with economy-crippling cost-of-living-adjustments, and then get out of Dodge.

Then you have the final 20 percent. They are the worst. All they want to do is advance themselves while doing as little as possible. They lie, steal, and cheat for the greater good of . . . themselves. They continually corrupt and manipulate the system to the detriment of the other 80 percent. And guess what? They couldn't care less. I'm willing to bet you know a few people from each category.

So in life, the trick as an employer is to find those first 20 percent, hire them, and then keep them happy.

If you are poor, you need to do all you can to get in, and then remain in, that first 20 percent. Hard work, decency, street smarts, and persistence will conquer a lot of ills.

4

Ignorance and the Poor

Ignorance in any form is dangerous. Ignorance is especially destructive among the poor, for some fairly obvious reasons.

While it is most certainly true that we are all ignorant about some things, the poor of our nation—mostly because almost every minute of their day is filled with the tasks needed just to survive—have little or no time to educate themselves about things that may eventually lighten the burden of their plight. Such is the paradox of their everyday existence. They are in the most need of education and the tools needed to escape poverty, yet almost always have neither the time nor the funds to get them. It is a catch-22 that can, and tragically does, have devastating results.

Ignorance breeds *evil* pure and simple. I know that is a strong word, but until you have seen the pain, suffering, and destruction caused by ignorance, you cannot truly understand. And worst of all, it affects the children of the poor more than the parents. It also has a huge impact on single moms.

It bothers me when academics and liberals—one and the same in most cases—discuss poverty but only want to talk around the edges of the problem, and almost always make excuses for *all* below the poverty line.

Such politically correct oversimplifications and cover-ups only serve to undermine the vast majority of the poor of our nation who strictly adhere to the rules of God, the rules of law, and civilized conduct in general as they desperately fight to carve out a better life for themselves and especially their children.

The truth that these liberals and academics purposefully ignore is that *some* below the poverty line are the absolute worst of the worst and have *only* themselves to blame for their predicament.

Some liberals and academics don't like to discuss this truth because they think it may reflect disproportionately on minority America. That flawed and, in fact, biased thinking is a form of racism. They forget that the majority of poor in our nation are white Americans. For many liberals and for many in the mainstream media, poor white Americans don't exist. Or if they do, they are less deserving of help or understanding than minorities who happen to be poor.

Look, trash is trash. You have the trash you take to the curb for the garbageman to collect. And then you have the trash who may live next door to you, or is even part of your family.

We've all heard the expression "He's just white trash. He don't know no better." Well, aside from the fact that the accuser clearly needs a better education, the reality is that there is also "*black* trash," "*brown* trash" and "*yellow* trash."

These human beings are "trash" not because they are poor, but because they are ignorant and often become a threat to civilized society. And this ignorance, much like a genetic DNA code, all but condemns them and their children to a life of misery.

I can't tell you how many times I've seen human "trash"—white, black, brown—turn to their five-year-old child and scream, "Shut the f--- up! What the f--- did I just tell you! You don't touch that f---ing candy until we get home." Once the tirade is over, the child is then usually slapped, punched, or shaken.

It happens *all* the time among the ignorant poor. Inner-city minority or rural white, it does not matter. This crime against our most young and innocent has nothing to do with skin color and everything to do with ignorance and a reluctance by many in government, the media, and even entertainment to confront and challenge such ignorance.

What greater accomplishment is there in life than literally saving the lives and the very futures of young children? Even if it's just one child.

Time and time again I've seen this disgusting behavior, and time and time again I've basically cried with the thought, *That child's life is over. At five years of age, because of the evil ignorance that spews out of his parent, his life is doomed.*

While on this subject, I have a news flash for the rich, yuppie parents who are too busy with their *important* careers to take proper care of their very pampered children. The evilness of ignorance is touching the lives of *your* children as well. You are just not aware of it yet, as you climb out of your BMW and head to the law firm, the country club, or Neiman Marcus.

As an all-too-real example, while on a walk through Lafayette Park in Washington, D.C., I witnessed and confronted both examples of ignorance up close.

As I was strolling through the park on my daily walk for fresh air, exercise, and thinking time, I saw two young black women in their early twenties with about twelve very well-dressed three- and four-year-old white boys and girls.

The two young black women were part of a day-care center, and they had taken the twelve little white boys and girls out for a walk. Or a push in this case. All of the little boys and girls were sitting in these very cool red wooden strollers, and each had three benches for the kids to sit.

Each kid looked like he or she had just stepped out of the pages of a catalogue for Baby Gap or Gap Kids.

Knowing D.C. and that particular area, I was guessing that most of the parents of these children were lawyers who made between $150,000 and $800,000 plus per year. Should *both* parents be lawyers, well then, "Fire up the Bentley, and let's send our kid to the 'best' day-care center in D.C."

But is it the best? Really?

With all of their money and self-anointed power, how do they really know? If it were a client instead of their child, they would investigate the day-care center and its employees eight ways to Sunday. But since it's *only* their own flesh and blood, why bother. I mean, after all, they do have those cool strollers so they *must* be good. Right?

Allow me to enlighten these rich white folks who would prefer to have others raise their children while they go to jobs they have fooled themselves into thinking somehow mean something in the grand scheme of things. They don't. Your *children* mean something. In fact, they should mean *everything*.

As I'm walking past these adorable, well-dressed kids, I hear both of the young black women loudly firing the F-bomb at each other as they smoked within breathing distance of the children. Not nice.

Several thoughts went through my mind as I walked past. The first was that those "adorable" kids just heard all of that and most likely hear it on a regular basis. The second thought was that these two black women were themselves the *by-products* of ignorance. Years before, their parent or parents had spoken to them the exact same way, and now that is how they speak to each other and the world around them. They not only had no respect for these children or their job, but no respect for themselves or each other.

I thought again about the parents of these twelve little rich white kids. Why didn't they at least take the time to observe those in charge of their precious children from afar? Oh, what they would have learned. They surely would have done such due diligence for their client or law firm. Don't their *own* kids merit the same attention to detail or better?

My last thought of the moment was, *I just can't let that go. I've got to go back and say something.*

My penchant for *not* letting things go tended to create problems for me at home. My wife—like most "normal" people—preferred to ignore bad things or have someone else deal with them. At least most of the time.

Human nature often tells us not to get involved. It's not *our* problem, so let someone else deal with it. Let's just keep walking and get away from the trouble as fast as possible.

That *is* human nature, and it's "normal"—and I guess it's sometimes good advice. But it's good advice I have never taken for myself.

As I see it, one of the major problems facing our nation, and especially the poor of our nation, is that nobody wants to get involved. *Nobody.*

And because nobody wants to get involved, mostly bad things happen. Very bad things. And these bad things happen because good people choose to ignore the evil before them and purposefully look the other way.

I have always been struck by the quote shared by Pastor Martin Niemöller with the United States Congress in 1968:

> *They came first for the Communists,*
> *and I didn't speak up because I wasn't a Communist.*
> *Then they came for the trade unionists,*
> *and I didn't speak up because I wasn't a trade unionist.*
> *Then they came for the Jews,*
> *and I didn't speak up because I wasn't a Jew.*
> *Then they came for me*
> *and by that time no one was left to speak up.*

Our country and the world in general are on a collision course with this indifference and selfishness. Every day we spiral down further and further into an abyss of ignoring those who need our help, while running and hiding from the trouble.

"We are our brother's keeper" sounds great when read from the Bible or heard in the movies. In real life, however, too many of us turn our back on those in need as we dash into our homes, lock the doors, and pretend.

Well, for better or worse, I actually do believe that we are our brother's keeper. If not us, then who?

Forget the self-serving dreck uttered by some televangelists with multimillion-dollar homes and private jets. Just ask yourself the always relevant question, "What would Jesus do?" What would *your* God do? If you are a nonbeliever, then "What is the right thing to do?"

We pretend that the evil is not out there or that if it is, at the very least it won't come to get us. It will only attack our neighbors or our friends but not us, because we chose to hide from its destruction. Wrong.

We are *all* on the list, and if we don't stand up for ourselves and offer a hand of support to those most at risk, then the evil will get us as well. It's just a matter of time.

In a somewhat ironic twist but on this same topic, several months earlier I had a confrontation in this *exact* same park. A park that is right across the street from the White House.

It was just a few weeks after the terrorist attacks of September 11, 2001. I was walking through the park on my way to a meeting in the White House. As I was walking on one of the redbrick paths of the park, I walked past a Middle Eastern–looking man—politically incorrect to say, I know, but accurate—bent over a pile of something in the grass.

The realization of *what* he was doing was a delayed reaction. As I walked about twenty feet farther on, the understanding of what he was up to hit me.

Right there in Lafayette Park—in full view of the White House, the Secret Service, and the Park Police positioned on Pennsylvania

Avenue—this guy was attempting to burn a large number of small American flags.

I stopped in my tracks, turned around, and screamed, "Hey!" He looked up at me but stayed down on one knee as he moved the flame from his Bic lighter back and forth across the cloth of the flags.

As I was headed toward the White House for a meeting with a friend of mine, I was dressed in a suit. Again, one of the suits made for me in Venezuela. To demonstrate how much I really did fear an additional browbeating from my wife, the thought honestly crossed my mind that she would be less than pleased with me if I got dirt or, worse yet, blood on my suit.

Of course, I had that thought as I was charging full-blast at this guy. It bears repeating that because of the just-completed terrorist attacks, everyone's nerves were on edge at the time. Mine were no different.

Just as he stood up from the now-burning flags, I put my right shoulder into him and he went flying across the grass. When he stood up, he stared at me for a second in a rage, then ran as fast as he could toward the Sixteenth Street exit of the park.

Knowing he was of no worry, I looked down at the burning flags. The only thing I could think to do was to try and stomp the fire out with my feet. As I was doing this, the sole of my right shoe actually caught on fire. There was now a *flame* coming from the bottom of my right shoe. As I continued to stomp, I laughed with the thought of what this must look like to a passerby.

A few more stomps and I had extinguished the fire on the flags and the bottom of my shoe. The flags were ruined. I took what was left of the red, white, and blue cloth and gently placed it in a trash container next to the path.

As I was doing that, I wondered why no one from the Secret Service or Park Police had come over. Luckily, this guy was only burning flags that day and not trying to launch a TOW missile or a rocket-propelled grenade at the White House.

Leaving those thoughts aside, I realized I still had to get to my meeting in the White House. As I double-timed it across Pennsylvania Avenue, the now-burned sole of my right shoe stuck to the pavement as I walked. A quick flashback to my flopping sole as a child hit me as I crossed the famous street.

When I finally cleared into the office of my friend Christopher Henick—Chris was, at the time, deputy assistant to President George W. Bush and helped take charge in the Situation Room on the morning of 9/11—he looked up at me as he twitched his nose and asked, "What's that burning smell?"

Back to the little rich white kids. As I walked back to the two young black women who were sitting on one of the park's green wooden benches, I already knew the outcome of what was about to happen. I knew the outcome but still felt a need to say what I thought.

I stood in front of one of the women who had used the foul language. "Why would you talk like that in front of these children?"

She wouldn't even look up at me as she took a drag on her cigarette. "What," she asked.

"Why would you swear like that in front of these kids? Don't you care that those words are very destructive?"

This time she did look up at me. She let loose with a barrage of F-bombs and told me to get my "white a--" out of her sight.

Fortunately, most of the kids were now playing in the grass and out of earshot. I decided to be clever with my parting shot.

"Doesn't it bother you that you are perpetuating the worst kind of stereotype?"

She once again refused to look at me. "Per . . . What?" she asked in confusion.

As I walked away, I looked over my shoulder and said, "Buy a dictionary and then go finish your GED."

Right on cue, just as if we had rehearsed it, she fired her last and loudest F-bomb at me.

Right there in Lafayette Park, just feet from the White House, was a prime example of the dangers of ignorance and poverty. The two young black women—who deserved and deserve every chance for happy and productive lives—were themselves products of ignorance and became what they saw and were subjected to growing up.

Coupled with that was the ignorance of the rich white parents who turned their babies over to women like this. The damage caused by ignorance knows no bounds. It is pervasive. It is relentless and all-consuming if we don't fight back.

The worst of all ignorance is the ignorance practiced by the rich and powerful. They think they can remain safe and untouched in their $800,000 homes and gated communities.

This very same ignorance is spreading like a disease among our lawmakers on Capitol Hill. They willingly ignore the plight of their very own poor constituents, for reasons already stated. "The poor don't vote, they don't come from my world of affluence, and I never have any contact with them; so maybe they don't exist."

Human nature tells us to run and hide from problems or bad things. Well, human nature is wrong. The more we run and hide, the worse it is going to get for all of us. Including members of Congress.

Civilized society is unraveling at the seams because of a lack of faith and morals and because some willingly twist their faith in the name of evil. As this transpires, many stand on the sidelines watching it happen and praying that *someone else* will take care of the problem.

Keep dreaming and keep hiding under your bed, because that is never going to happen. Evil is coming, and you are on the list.

Do something about it.

The Lord may help us. But only if we help ourselves. Get up and take a stand.

5

Political Correctness and Affirmative Action—Enemies of the Poor

Political correctness is a creation of liberals and "poverty pests"—those who make their wealth on the backs of the poor and ignorant—to make themselves feel better while doing nothing to help the poor and disenfranchised. In fact, it ultimately hurts them more than it helps.

Political correctness *separates* people. It underscores the differences between races and then tells one group, "We are going to treat you with different rules because you are *anything* but a white male. And because we have underscored your differences to society, we are going to *tell* society that there is a different rule-book in effect for you because . . . well . . . because I guess you're not as good as a white male and need help. You need *our* help. The help of liberal white people."

Political correctness is the enemy of the poor and it is the enemy of minorities. As is affirmative action. Affirmative action is just another way of saying that as a society, we have failed minority Americans, and so to make up for our failures, we are going to give minority Americans special breaks and privileges that will ultimately cause them to fall even further behind white America as well as—and this is critically important—immigrant minorities.

As an example, let's look at affirmative action and the role it plays in college admissions—colleges that, by the way, regularly discriminate against conservative and Christian thought.

Liberals want and insist on using race and ethnicity as factors for gaining admission to a college. They are willing to use these factors at the expense of good grades and qualifications. Why?

Some liberals will tell you that diversity is needed on our college campuses and that such exposure will broaden the horizons of all students . . . even the white ones. Could be. But at what cost to those minority students who are allowed to get in with bad grades and then flunk out after one semester or one year? What helping hand were they *really* given by affirmative action? Do these liberals bother to track the rate of minority students who drop out of college or flunk out because they can't handle the academics? Do they track the aftereffects of this social engineering gone wrong?

I am *not* trying to be partisan here. This is too important a subject to be cheapened by partisanship. I am merely asking an honest question that needs to be answered—honestly.

Do those who selfishly and ignorantly push affirmative action actually bother to track the plight of these pawns on the chessboard of liberal ideology?

These are young human beings with but one life to live. Not faceless statistics to be used to score partisan debating points.

Do you want to know *why* the left does not like to publicize or acknowledge the dropout rate of these young people? Because they know the truth and are terrified to have it revealed. That truth is that many *public* school teachers who "educated" these minority students in K–12 are a disgrace and have failed their students miserably.

But guess what? As stressed earlier—and it really can't be screamed about enough—most liberals will never accuse public school teachers of being *bad* teachers, because the teachers and the teachers' unions happen to bankroll the Democratic Party and support the candidates that the liberals love. So rather than solve the problem and *save* some of these children, some liberals would rather cover up for these disgustingly bad public school teachers and throw the kids overboard. Certain liberals want and need racial preferences in college to cover up for the failures of bad public school teachers as well as their own failed social engineering.

In the United States of today, less than half of African-American and Hispanic-American ninth graders in public school will graduate from high school. Less than half. *That* is the legacy of political correctness and affirmative action. They fail to solve the education gap of minorities, while *creating* more poverty-stricken Americans.

In my mind, treating someone differently and giving them preferential treatment because they are a minority is flat-out *racism*.

African-American and Hispanic-American students represent proud cultures that have contributed more than can be counted to the greatness of our nation. Much more than the liberals who seek to keep them down.

6

What's So Wrong with Hard Work?

For those who continually push for a free ride and entitlements for everyone, I have a question: What's so wrong with good old-fashioned hard work and personal responsibility?

Be it California, Greece, or the United States, *somebody* has to work. *Somebody* has to pay for everything. *Somebody* has to create jobs. *Somebody* has to create opportunity.

And for all those things to happen, *somebody* has to be honest and admit that the free-ride policies advocated by certain politicians, most in the mainstream media, and most in academia are destroying our free-market system and any chance for the poor to escape their almost always undeserved existence.

Look, as most of us know, life is very, very hard and getting tougher with each passing day. To better deal with that reality, we need to understand that no one is *owed* a job. No one is *owed* a home. No one is *owed* a higher education, and no one is *owed* unlimited outs in pee-wee baseball or T-ball.

Other than liberty—in all of its traditional values manifestations—we are not entitled to anything. Period.

That said, the growing demands for entitlements by many on the left is creating a nation of unprepared and soft adults followed by a backbench of wimpy, whiny, spoiled, fat kids.

The late-great comedian Richard Pryor spoke to this effect; I'll shorten and clean up what he said. He joked that the reason Japan bombed Pearl Harbor to start World War II was that before the war, many of the Japanese leadership had attended elite colleges in California and found them populated by rich, pampered, wimpy, entitled students who barely had the strength to carry their own books, let alone fight someone.

The Japanese leadership remembered those wimps and collectively said, "Ah, we can beat those skinny country-club kids in a war."

Pryor then joked that right after Pearl Harbor, the United States unchained and unleashed its incredibly tough, snarling, football-playing, "unsophisticated" students from places like the University of Alabama and the University of Georgia, and it was soon lights out for the Japanese.

There are a number of solid lessons in the story and joke, not the least of which is that we always need to be prepared, and we always need to understand that the world and life do not play by our increasingly soft and politically correct rules. Certain countries and certain ruthless leaders do believe in survival of the fittest and that any and all measures can be employed in life, in business, and especially in war.

Life *is* hard. People, countries, and terrorists play dirty. Like it or not, there are still winners and losers. And often victory still goes to the toughest, most prepared kid on the team.

Deal with it or pay the consequences.

Whatever the actual number is, the reality is that there are millions of Americans who are touched by and suffer greatly from the unrelenting effects of poverty. As such, it's crucial that they understand that hard work and personal responsibility are *the* keys to escape the shackles.

Knowing the right thing to do is never tough. Never. Doing

the right thing at exactly the right time for exactly the right reasons is very tough. Always.

As we contemplate that truth, we would do well to remember the oft-quoted line attributed to John Bradford from the 1500s: "There but for the grace of God go I."

7

Never Afraid of the Abyss

An ironic positive that comes from real poverty is that it creates a willingness to take chances and roll the dice. For me, it is one of the real life-altering positives to come out of the whole ugly and destructive experience.

Over the last number of years, I have been asked numerous times how I got out of that lifestyle and became a "success."

I am bothered by the fact that some asking the question are defining "success" as having money. Because I somehow managed to become "wealthy" in their minds, that classifies me as a "success." Nothing could be further from the truth.

My *only* definition of success is someone who lives his or her life to the best of his or her abilities while remaining a good and decent person. A successful life for me is imbued with faith, family, friends, and it uses that Golden Rule as a moral compass.

Money has absolutely nothing to do with it. As Johnny Carson once very wisely observed, "Money gives you the luxury of not having to worry about money." Very true. Having money may free up your mind from some worry but it does *not* define success or happiness.

The reality and irony for me was that a complete *lack* of money gave me an inner strength that many contemporaries of mine, including friends and relatives, did not have.

Abject poverty provided me with an unbeatable ace in the hole. I was not afraid to fail. *I was not afraid to try.* I was not afraid to be embarrassed. And I was not afraid to start over if I fell on my face—which was often.

I *knew* what bad and sometimes evil things lay in the darkness waiting for me if I failed. I knew what they were, but I was not afraid of them. I hated that situation but I was not remotely panicked. For what awaited failure was simply more poverty, more uncertainty, and more pain. *So what?* I didn't want to be homeless again, but I was not going to let fear of the unknown or failure keep me from following my particular path. All the opposite. Those things *kept* me on my path.

Growing up, while we did have loving and caring relatives, there were a few who quite cruelly looked down upon me, my sister, and my brother. Even though our poverty, our uncleanness, and our lot in life was not remotely our fault, these relatives thought of us as less than them and most certainly less than their children. And they happily vocalized such beliefs to others in the family . . . and always when I, my brother, and sister were in earshot.

While a desire to prove these unenlightened relatives wrong was certainly a motivating factor, the main reason I escaped the cesspool and became financially independent was . . . drumroll please . . . that I didn't care what others thought. I didn't care about the excuses. I didn't care who had more than me. I cared *only* about the next few minutes, hours, and days and how I was going to survive it all.

I had many, many days when I had no home, no food, hadn't bathed in weeks, and had no idea what degree of pain tomorrow would bring. Only that if the sun came up, then the pain was a certainty.

Every single day of my childhood was painted and framed in such misery. Most people, my relatives and friends included, never have *one* of those days. No doubt they have all had their share of bad days. But most have never had the off-the-chart bizarre days that had become the norm for me, Jay, and Janice.

Do not misunderstand me. As a child and young adult, if I could have switched places with my cousins or better-off schoolmates, I would have done so in a second. To live in a world of clean clothes, three meals a day, a permanent nice home, the same school, and a foundation for a future would have been all of our dreams rolled into one.

A few times after staying with my cousins for a week down in Maryland, we would return to Boston only to find out that our family had just been evicted from the home we had *just left* to go on our trip. Insane.

If you meet someone in life who has escaped real poverty, I can promise you one thing: that person learned at a young age how to compartmentalize things . . . especially pain. For the truth is, if you come from that world and you *don't* learn this trick, then most likely you won't survive. And if you do manage to survive, then you almost certainly don't prosper.

Politics aside, people always wonder how Bill Clinton excelled in so many aspects of life when he came from a childhood of extreme dysfunction. Simply put, he learned the trick. He locked the bad into little compartments within his mind and dealt with them at the times best suited for him, his temperament, and his environment.

Agree with him or not. Like him or not. The fact that he made himself a member of the most exclusive club in the world was not an accident. Affirmative action played no role. Early on, it was all on him.

To be sure, once he crossed the first threshold into elective politics, the mainstream media and the liberal intelligentsia lent him a hand—often unethically—whenever and wherever possible. But before he crossed that threshold, he had to make it or break it based on his talent and his ability to lock away the pain and unimagined dysfunction.

Some conservatives and some Republicans—maybe most—refuse to give President Clinton credit for *anything* or acknowledge *any* talent, skill, or determination. I happen to think they are wrong.

I respect his accomplishment and his intellect; and I respect and, more important, understand what he overcame as a child and young man. The rest? That's between him and God.

Because of poverty, I'd never been afraid to try new things. By the age of thirteen, I had developed a fairly low opinion of my fellow man and didn't believe anyone was "better" than me. The only reason, in my mind, that they had more money and opportunities was that they were either born into it or were given the foundation to go out and do it. Whatever "do it" was for them.

So I decided, and in fact made it a part of my very being, that I would not be afraid to go after anything or any job that I wanted. I decided this, because I knew I had an ace in the hole: complete failure would not defeat me nor kill me. I knew that if I lost everything and ended up living in a Kenmore refrigerator box, I would still be okay. I certainly did not want to be in that situation again but was not remotely afraid of the poverty or that outcome.

This may sound somewhat strange or unbelievable to most, but in many ways during those difficult years, abject poverty was like an old friend. There was a comfort level to the poverty. I knew that environment and knew the rules of the game. The only real rule was simply to survive.

The reverse of that was the lesson I learned. I've watched friends and others settle. Settle because the fear of the unknown was more powerful than the desire to chase their dreams.

Oftentimes people who come from secure, middle-class, or even upper-middle-class homes have a fear of the unknown. A fear of taking chances. A fear of taking the leap of a lifetime—afraid they will miss the branch and fall down into the black and bottomless abyss of "failure."

Ironically, security, a wonderful home life, and "normalcy" can make some risk-averse. *Very* risk-averse. Much better to always straddle that fence, put in thirty years, get the gold watch, and retire in Florida. Follow the tried-and-true road map and leave the dream-chasing to others.

Except . . . we only get *one* or *two* real chances in a lifetime to chase and obtain the dream. Be that dream a job, a vocation, a spouse, or the creative arts. This life is all we have on earth and unless you come from that privileged, out-of-touch, pampered elite, no one is *ever* going to hand you your dream.

You have to fight for it, and at certain times even throw caution to the wind.

During my life, I've failed at more things than I have succeeded at. But I have no regrets. Regrets only add fuel to the fire that is sadness, loneliness, and pain. I had been handed most of the ingredients for that recipe as a child and had no intention of adding "regret" to the list.

8

That's All . . . for Now

I have told you enough here about my life, my issues, and my ideas. Ultimately, I wanted to shine some light on the problems of those living in poverty from the perspective of one who has been there. I tried to do so while maintaining a sense of integrity, reality, and a little humor. I hope I have succeeded in some small way.

In closing, if I may be bold enough to leave you with some truly heartfelt advice forged in the fires of my life, it would be this:

"Wake up. Get up. Do something. Make *your* gifts count."

May God bless you and may God bless us all.

ACKNOWLEDGMENTS

First and above all, I would like to thank my sister, Janice Ovide (O-Vee-Dee), and my brother, Jay MacKinnon, for all their love over the years. I especially want to thank them for their enthusiastic support of this memoir. As mentioned, my childhood experiences were for the most part *their* childhood experiences. At times, it was a very emotional and painful process for me to remember and then articulate certain periods of our life. During those times, it was comforting to speak with the only two people on earth who shared those unpleasant memories and have a good cry.

With that process in mind, I'd also like to thank my brother, Jay, for his help as I hustled to meet my deadline.

Next, I would like to thank Lacy Lalene Lynch and everyone at Dupree-Miller for their belief in me and this project and my buddy Ken Abraham for pointing me in their direction. Thanks to them, I have been most fortunate to work with Howard Books and the entire Simon & Schuster family.

With Philis Boultinghouse, I have been blessed with an amazing editor, an incredibly good and decent person, and a kindred spirit. She is the best. So, as they say, whatever boo boos found in the book are the fault of the moronic author and no one else.

From that Howard Books and Simon & Schuster family, I'd also like to thank Amanda Demastus, Susan Wilson, Jennifer Smith, Ashley Earnhardt, and Stephanie Evans for their many efforts to make this a better and ultimately successful book, with extra-special kudos going to Amanda for her nonstop assistance and support.

While I'm at it, I'd like to acknowledge the spectacular voice and immense talent of Michelle Wright. She hails from my second home country of Canada and her CDs—along with those of Mr. Frank Sinatra—were playing often in the background while I scribbled.

Finally, and as always, I'd like to thank Patrick Ryan Ovide (O-Vee-Dee) for his constant love and inspiration and for being my best friend in the whole wide universe.

Printed in the United States
By Bookmasters